TEACHING RECEPTION

Ms Uddington

Edited by Lucy Hall

Published by Scholastic Ltd.
Villiers House
Clarendon Avenue
Leamington Spa
Warwickshire CV32 5PR
Text © 1998 Paul Noble; George Hunt; Peter Clarke; Terry Jennings;
Margaret Mackintosh; Dorothy Tipton; Gillian Robinson; Pauline Boorman; Richard Ager;
Lynn Newton; Doug Newton; Geoffrey Teece
© 1998 Scholastic Ltd.

7 8 9 0   2 3 4 5 6 7

Authors

Paul Noble, George Hunt, Peter Clarke, Terry Jennings, Margaret Mackintosh,
Dorothy Tipton, Gillian Robinson, Pauline Boorman, Richard Ager, Lynn Newton,
Doug Newton, Geoffrey Teece

Series Editor
Lucy Hall

Editor
Jane Bishop

Series Designer
Lynne Joesbury

Designer
Anna Oliwa

Illustrations
Jenny Mumford

Cover photograph
Fiona Pragoff

Designed using Adobe Pagemaker

British Library Cataloguing-in-Publication Data
A catalogue record for this book is available from the British Library

ISBN 0 590 53818 7

The publishers acknowledge and thank the following for the use of copyright material:
National Curriculum 2000 © The Queen's Printer and Controller of HMSO. Reproduced under the terms of HMSO Guidance Note 8. © Qualifications and Curriculum Authority. Reproduced under the terms of Guidance Note 8. *National Literacy and Numeracy Documents* © Crown Copyright. Reproduced under the terms of HMSO Guidance Note 8. *Early Learning Goals* © Qualifications and Curriculum Authority.

Contents

Preface

Primary school teachers don't say, as secondary teachers would, 'I teach history'. They say 'I teach year 4s' or 'I teach a reception class'. Why, then, have all the books for primary teachers been wholly subject-orientated? Primary teachers have had to buy about 13 different books and read through them all to extract the relevant bits.

It was about 20 years ago, that the thought occurred to me that it would make teachers' lives much easier if all the information about teaching their year group was provided in *one* book. Since then I have been waiting for someone to do it. But no one did. So, finally, fourteen different authors, Scholastic and I have put together the seven *Primary Teacher Yearbooks*.

I should like to thank all the authors. They faced a difficult task in tailoring their writing to a common format and structuring their guidance, about what to teach and what to expect from children, so that it correlated with the seven different stages of the primary school. They have all been extremely patient.

Particular thanks are due to Paul Noble, who not only wrote 13 chapters in the series, but was also deeply involved in the development of the project from the very beginning. His practical, knowledgeable advice and cheerful imperturbability kept the whole project stuck together.

We all hope that you will find your Yearbook useful and that it meets your needs – whichever class you teach.

Lucy Hall, Series Editor

Your Class

As the reception class teacher you have heavy responsibilities. You have to introduce the children to the world of school, help them to come to terms with living in a large social group, lay the foundations for learning in all the subjects of the primary curriculum – most crucially in maths and reading – and ensure that they come to school with enthusiasm and pleasure. It is physically and mentally exhausting and demanding, but most reception teachers would argue that it can also be the most rewarding of classes to teach.

Matching children and curriculum

The reception class covers the year in which children have their fifth birthdays. Approaches differ between schools and children may be admitted once a year, twice a year or even each term. Legally, they become of compulsory school age on September 1, January 1 or April 1 – whichever of these dates first follows their fifth birthday. However, at whatever time they are admitted, your class is still their introduction to real schooling.

The curriculum you teach in reception is the last year of the foundation stage and should be planned to help children make good progress towards or even beyond the early learning goals. The foundation stage ends at the end of reception year and the National Curriculum begins when children enter Year One.

Pre-admission and induction

Arrange preliminary visits for the children and their parents, to take place at the end of the term preceding their official entry date. This visit might take the form of:
- a brief morning visit with parents;
- a series of short, regular daily visits with nursery or playgroup;

- a formal long visit, perhaps half a morning, during which parents remain;
- a full half-day at school;
- an afternoon after-school session(s);
- casual morning visits (with prior notice) whenever parents choose during a designated week (parents staying with their child).

One good idea is to invite the new children to a 'Teddy bears' picnic' for half an hour after the normal school day.

Once children start school the induction process must continue. Consider these approaches:

- Stagger admission times. Try not to have more than six new entrants at a time, and admit the children at half-hourly intervals or spread the intake over several days during the first week of school.
- Avoid receiving new children just as the rest of the school is starting (this can be an intimidating experience).
- Allow parents to remain with their children for the first ten minutes or so.
- Start with half-day schooling. For children admitted very early in their fourth year, initial part-time schooling is essential (unless you have suitable equipment and facilities for this age group).

Early contact with parents and children

Although parents will have received a school brochure and formal letters of invitation, it is worth going further to welcome them and their children and to start some valuable communication. You could:

- Issue a booklet on 'How to help your child start school'. Include in it any data that has been missed out by the school brochure and give carers and parents some idea of what the school expects. For example, that children should be toilet trained, that they should have practised fastening buttons, holding a pencil, and changing for PE. Be wary of making parents feel inadequate, but reassure them that by loving their children, talking with them and listening to them, they are giving them the best possible start in school. Encourage them to read stories to their children and describe the sort of simple counting or recognition games that they might play in school.

- Send a letter or booklet of welcome to the children. Consider spending some money to provide photographs showing key things ('this is your teacher'; 'this is the classroom'; 'here are the toilets' and so on). Where a new entrant is non-English-speaking, such a booklet is invaluable. Use each child's name frequently (and correctly) as an additional link. If children are to join an existing class then you should include a picture of one of their classmates in the welcome booklet.
- Collect information from parents about children's pre-school experiences (illnesses; when they first walked; whether they attended playgroup). This data should form part of the school's baseline assessment procedure.

What to do during visits

During the children's first visits to you, give each child a chance to get used to you, learn your name, hear your voice and see you long enough to recognise you at a later date. Talk to them and get them to talk to you.

When they have got over the shock of arrival, familiarise the children with the geography of the classroom and some parts of the school. Consider involving older children to act as chaperones, pairing them with the younger children. Show them the places illustrated in your letter, making sure they know where the entrance is, where the toilets are and so on.

Let the children try out your facilities, hanging up their coats, using the toilets, perhaps even having a trial school lunch. Make sure they appreciate that classrooms are interesting places, with plenty of areas to explore.

Some children will prefer to be left alone to get used to you and to the new world in which they find themselves. Others will be keen to get involved so have construction toys, painting aprons and craft items ready for them to use.

When the children leave after their first induction visit, let them take something home with them. It may be a picture they have drawn or a model they have made. You might even provide a 'play pack' for each child, of activities to do at home (cutting out, drawing a picture, tracing letters, matching, colouring and so on).

Reassuring parents

For some parents this will be the first major act of separation since their child was born and they will need a chance to adjust to it. When the head teacher meets formally with parents before admission you should, of course, be present. Try to remember names and faces, if necessary making notes (parents don't usually mind) because they will expect you to remember that Isobel doesn't eat cheese or that Daniel always fights with Shane.

Important medical information and contact numbers will already have been noted on your school's admission form. However, the casual information that parents give you is very important to them, so take note.

Parents will be eager to trust you and will be looking for reassurance. You might explain briefly the school's approach to reading or number, to confirm your professional competence and help the parents understand what will be expected of their children. Make a display of books and materials which you use in reception for parents to browse through.

Parental contact during term time

Make the ground rules for parental contact clear, otherwise you will be overwhelmed by parents every morning just when the children themselves need you most.

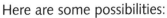

Here are some possibilities:

- in the morning – emergencies only (direct access to you);
- administrative queries about dinner money and so on (to the school office);
- discussion of immediate work problems (after school with you – by arrangement);
- general progress (by appointment).

One good idea is to have regular 'Parent clinics', for example on the first Tuesday every month after school, where parents can have the opportunity to discuss progress as well as problems. As a reception teacher you will get enormous interest and may be a little overwhelmed initially.

Receiving and dismissing children

How you receive the children each morning is important because it can affect your relationship with each child for the day, and will also colour how you are perceived by the parents.

First make sure that the reception entrance is clearly signposted together with your classroom, the cloakrooms and, of course, the school office. Imagine that you are a complete stranger approaching the building and you will soon see what is needed. If there are 'no go' areas for parents, then these should be clearly signposted, too. Vehicular and pedestrian access to the school should be organised and clearly communicated so that parents know what the rules are; car parking is a problem for many schools.

Receiving reception children requires at least two pairs of adult hands. You should be in the classroom before the children – any other arrangement is unprofessional. The following receiving routine is commonly used in schools where more than one class share an entrance.

Two teachers greet children at the door before entry. Parents and children are gently separated and parents who wish to enter with their children are deterred. Inside the cloakroom or classroom, another supervising adult (a welfare/classroom assistant or non-duty teacher) supervises children until joined by colleagues who are 'on the door'.

Starting the day routine

Most reception classes start the day something like this:

- entry, greeting;
- hang up coats and store lunch boxes;
- return reading books and so on;
- sit on the carpet for registration.

'Carpet time' is necessary to give children the opportunity to share news with you. Get the class to say a collective good morning (it is one way of marking the start of the school day and ensuring that everyone is paying attention) or you may prefer to greet the children individually when marking the register. So that 'Good morning, Jonah' elicits the response 'Good morning, Mrs Noble' and this gives public notice that you are aware of each child's presence. Most children enjoy these moments.

Home time

Dismissing the children at the end of the day is an issue about which parents often express concern, as they feel their child to be increasingly vulnerable in a threatening world. Depending upon your situation, children might stand by their tables before dismissal, put their chairs up or gather on the carpet. Whatever your routine is, it should become habit.

Some teachers exchange *Good afternoons* with their children and in church schools the end of day ritual usually involves an afternoon prayer. Children should then be released in groups.

During the first term, take children to the exit door (no more than six at a time) and release them into the hands of a collecting adult. It is a matter of judgement, but usually after about six weeks children will not need to be managed quite so tightly. Clearly a reception teacher on her own cannot manage dismissal effectively and in most schools it will require two adults.

Parents should have somewhere to wait outside (not too close to classroom windows or they will be both noisy and nosy!). You must not allow children to leave the school yard/playground unless they have been collected and they should know that they must return to the classroom if there is any problem. You may wish to remain visible in the yard until all of your children have gone home. If necessary, a teacher could be on 'gate duty' watching for all the children to leave the playground.

Every child should be able to recognise his collecting adult and long-term changes in collecting arrangements should have been notified to the school. In cases of doubt, especially if the child makes a fuss and refuses to go with an adult, the general rule is to release the child into the hands of the person who delivered him or her, if necessary retaining the child to check the facts. The head teacher should deal with these matters (they may involve child custody arguments).

Behaviour issues

Criers, kickers and screamers

Most children starting school do not cry when separated from their mum. Children who are used to the company of others, through going to nursery or playgroup, are less likely to have outbursts. Allowing parents to stay for a while if their child does cry can help, but eventually, of course, they will have to be persuaded to leave.

Fortunately, four-year-olds are easily distracted and you should soon be able to stem tears by involving the child with a toy or a game, or joining in a rhyme with the rest of the class. Keep the tone of your voice level and encouraging; don't get cross. Having a classroom assistant or helper on hand to give the crying child some individual attention also helps. Sit

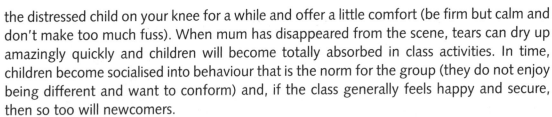

the distressed child on your knee for a while and offer a little comfort (be firm but calm and don't make too much fuss). When mum has disappeared from the scene, tears can dry up amazingly quickly and children will become totally absorbed in class activities. In time, children become socialised into behaviour that is the norm for the group (they do not enjoy being different and want to conform) and, if the class generally feels happy and secure, then so too will newcomers.

Occasionally you will come across persistent howlers, even children who are violent. Persistent extreme behaviour is invariably a sign that something is significantly wrong and, although the cause may lie in a personality or behaviour disorder, it is much more likely to have a social origin that lies outside the classroom. Possibly the child feels abandoned because of insecurity at home. Whatever the root of the problem, the school will need to work with parents to sort the matter out.

Happily extreme cases are rare, but be alert. All policies for dealing with suspicious cases are built on the premise that the child's interests are paramount. Suspected abuse must be reported.

Using the toilet

One of the baseline requirements for children entering formal schooling is that they should be fully toilet trained. It is rare, but not unknown, for perfectly normal children to arrive at school in nappies but, unless the child has a special physical need for which arrangements have been agreed, such a situation is unacceptable. The head teacher and even the GP may need to be brought in to advise the parents.

Children in reception should be able to go to the toilet whenever they need to. Unfortunately, it is not always easy to assess need and for some children 'going to the toilet' is a neat way to avoid work or to get up to mischief with a friend. Your classroom may be so positioned in relation to the lavatories, that keeping an eye on this sort of thing requires very little by way of a system. If you are not so lucky, you will need to establish a few ground rules.

Take children to the toilet (or invite them to go) as a matter of course before and after set activities – assembly or PE for example and insist that they visit the lavatory before going out to play or when they come back inside. During the less formal activities where the children are moving around the classroom and undertaking different activities, the rule might be that they simply go to the toilet without asking. During a more taught or set task, they must learn that permission is required.

One simple management technique is to have two sets of coloured bead necklaces, one for boys, one for girls, hanging close to the toilet or on the classroom door. Children must hang the appropriate necklace around their necks when going to the toilet and replace them on the hook on their return. By limiting the number of necklaces, there is an automatic control on the numbers allowed into the toilets at any one time and you can see at a glance whether there is anyone missing.

Keep a supply of clean underpants, knickers and shorts in case of accidents, and plastic bags for the dirties. In cases of soiling or illness the parents should be called to collect the child.

If a child is persistently smelly due to poor bladder control or lack of hygiene, then this must be dealt with via the parents, not the child. It is best to act straight away and get the parents to take remedial action. Treat the issue as commonplace but as something that, for the comfort of everybody, including the child, cannot be ignored.

Naughty and nice

'Reinforce the good rather than stress the bad' is sound advice whatever age-group you are teaching. Make sure that you have in place a simple reward system, perhaps merit stickers or stars. Allow children privileges when they have done something special or on occasions such as birthdays.

When bad behaviour occurs don't ignore it but make it clear what is and what is not acceptable. The very act of doing this is usually sufficient to modify behaviour and is part of the learning process. Bullying, pushing, swearing and even stealing are all things about which a young child has to learn. Although these matters should be taken seriously, they

A simple reward system, such as merit stickers, helps to reinforce good behaviour

are normal among young children and to be expected. Sometimes, especially when an aspect of behaviour has been given an emotive name, parents can over-react. For a four-year-old gradually learning to distinguish between what belongs to the class collectively and to him individually, 'theft' does not have quite the same meaning as it does for a habitual thief. You will need to explain this to some parents.

Keep a 'behaviour book' (you may prefer to call it a 'naughty book') and record incidents that give concern or repeated transgressions. This will help provide corroborating evidence if further action has to be taken.

How well your class behaves will depend a great deal on the general ethos of the school and on the tone you set in your classroom. 'Calm, positive and purposeful' are the three words that should guide your approach. Routines and systems help, but how you talk to and interact with children and other adults is more significant still.

Keeping attention

Young children clamour for attention, so establish some workable rules. You might like to use a visual signal that indicates you are not to be interrupted, for example:
- display a toy on your desk – 'Don't interrupt when the bear is there!';
- wear a particular piece of clothing – a different hat for each different purpose;
- use a sand-timer.

Children will enjoy observing the rules of the game. Perhaps, when they are seated on the carpet, it could become a magic and silent one.

Make your method of demanding attention explicit, for example, two hand claps means 'stop what you are doing'. Choose your method or you may become stuck with a less elegant habit like 'Er..!' or 'Excuse me!' (both used by colleagues who shall remain nameless).

Changing for PE

This can be a time-consuming nightmare if not handled properly. Be clear about what children should change into whether it be leotards, shorts, T-shirts, knickers, pumps, plimsolls or whatever. Decide how strict you will be about suitable clothing; will you permit printed T-shirts or not?

When the children are changing, have at least one other pair of adult hands to help. Undertake the changing process in steps, for the first few lessons the children might only undo the top button and take off ties, sweaters and shoes. Next, when they are able to

Stick a pair of old plimsolls, sprayed silver, on a board and encourage children to practise tying their shoelaces.

cope, you can extend this to changing an item of clothing and so on. Be patient but persist, and if children reveal that they never dress or undress themselves, it is time to have a word with their parents! Remember your children will not know what 'changing for PE' means and some will be stark naked in a trice if they are not properly instructed.

Playtimes and lunchtimes

Reception children do not mix easily with large numbers of older ones in a confined space and, for some timid children, time in the playground may even be a hated ordeal. During the first week or so it is best for you to be on hand and visible during playtimes and lunchtimes. Your new charges should not feel abandoned, and it is helpful if you are there to cut up difficult food and open yoghurt cartons.

Some children will go home to lunch, some will have sandwiches, and some will eat a cooked school lunch and you cannot expect four- and five-year-olds to remember what they are doing each day. Make lists of each category and use adult help to sort the children into groups. Disorientated children will panic, some will think it is home time and others will adopt lunch boxes that are not theirs. Be organised or problems will multiply! Be aware of the language you use; the question *Are you a dinner?* completely confuses some children (not surprisingly).

Inform midday supervisors about children who need special attention, for example, children who need to use a ventilator for their asthma. During lunchbreak keep a careful eye on children by themselves as well as the over-excited ones. Reception children do not usually make close friends but rather they play together, separately. Designating a quiet play area from which chasing games or older children are excluded is a good idea, as is a naughty wall to which miscreants have to stick for 'time out'.

It is not usually advisable to encourage children to bring small toys to school, on the other hand, it is best if they have something to do at playtimes! Discarded PE equipment is useful and midday supervisors can help organise skipping or simple singing games. Lines on the playground, hopscotch and balls all contribute to trouble-free playtimes.

The solution to wet playtimes and lunchtimes is simple – lots to do and adequate supervision. Think your wet playtime procedure through carefully, the extra effort is worth it in the long run. Have you got a special games or comics box? Is the supervision adequate?

Assemblies and celebrations

Many schools exclude their youngest children from full school assemblies for the first two or three weeks, which can be very confusing to reception children. But routines of celebration will soon be learned and enjoyed and children can become very upset when routines (good work assemblies, birthday assemblies, special playtime routines, changing the calendar, recording the weather and so on) are broken. When planning your first term, take account of school traditions such as Harvest Festival, the visit of the school photographer and so on.

It's a long day – falling asleep

By mid-afternoon some children have had enough of school and are ready for a nap. Others, presumably with atomic power sources, seem to be able to go on for ever.

If a child shows signs of falling asleep then accept it as a need which must be met. Make sure that he or she is comfortable (head down on a table, on a cushion or on the carpet) and that they will not accidentally hurt themselves. Most often sleep is induced during the end-of-the-day story (don't be offended) and a good tip is to get the other children to tip-toe round the sleeping child and then bring in the waiting parent. This is the best way to avoid a rude awakening.

Making progress

Reception is not only about starting – it is about moving on. Your children will start changing on day one. It is not unusual to get comments from parents after even a few days about how their child has changed (not always for the better!). This is inevitable as they learn to live in a large group with a new set of rules.

Perhaps one of the biggest lessons that children learn quickly, is that they cannot command your attention all the time. Voices have to be controlled and conventions have to be observed. Explain that *Just because you say 'Excuse me' doesn't mean that you can interrupt.*

Within a few weeks children will know what it means to 'line up', what 'playtime' is and so on. They will also broadly know what you expect of them. A month into the year and they will hardly be recognisable as the children who started. Much of this learning is to do with coping in a group and, as the months pass, your children will become more inhibited. A four-year-old starting school might shout out in class or in a whole school assembly *My mum's got a red dress!* when observing the clothes you are wearing, but by the end of the year, most would not dream of doing so. The process of socialisation has begun.

Hand-eye skills and academic skills will also be acquired but the changes here are more gradual and less dramatic. Even a Year 1 child still needs some help getting ready for PE and will have to be reminded to put on a coat. Academic progress is steady but sometimes unpredictable. Some – perfectly normal – children may not have moved very far along the road to becoming independent readers, whereas others will have made astonishing progress.

By the second term, the class should be able to cope with bigger social occasions, such as assemblies, and may take part in a class assembly before the year is out. Christmas productions may pose a challenge, but can usually be done in conjunction with older infants.

As with the learning of academic skills, social skills are not acquired by magic. A reception teacher's lot is to repeat and repeat again basic rules and strategies. Children have to be taught how to clear up – you cannot simply tell them to do it and expect it to happen, but need to specify the tasks individually – *Collect all the scissors*. They have to learn how to share and play and work together. All sorts of factors are involved here including home circumstances, siblings, habit and their nursery or playgroup experiences. You have to establish the pattern of behaviour that you want. Give these matters time (just as you will with the teaching of reading) for, without the right social training, other forms of learning will be made so much harder for the children.

At the end of their time with you, most children will have climbed well up the ladder of learning in maths and language, they will have acquired social habits that will stand them in good stead in the years ahead and they will be recognisably a group of biddable school children – as opposed to the group of self-centred, anarchic creatures that they were when they entered the school.

Specify tasks clearly, for example 'Collect all the scissors'

Curriculum and Classroom Planning

Your school will probably impose a standardised planning sheet on you. One way of covering the prescribed curriculum, whether it is the early learning goals or the National Curriculum, is to think first in terms of topics then of the activities you intend the children to carry out. Plan for the whole class and for groups across the whole year group, whether the children are under or over five-years-old. Then simply identify the area of learning and the early learning goal to which each activity relates.

You will, of course, need to check at some point the areas covered against the curriculum documents to make sure nothing has been missed. For example, you will need to check your coverage of literacy against the National Literacy Strategy and your coverage of mathematics against the National Numeracy Strategy, in addition to the Early Learning Goals (QCA) for all six areas of learning. Because of the tight dovetailing of these documents you will find few gaps to fill. You can, of course, start the process the other way round and work from the agendas to the activities but, because you have a mixture of prescriptions – and children, it is generally easier the other way round.

Knowing your children, and indeed yourself, you will inevitably come up with detailed solutions to classroom-planning issues that may vary from the suggestions given here, but the principles followed should be the same.

Think in terms of these three headings: Place, Time and Materials/Resources. To some extent these headings are arbitrary and they are certainly interlinked, but gathering your thoughts under headings like these should prevent you from trying to think about too many things at once.

Place

The secret of a good classroom is that the space is arranged in such a way that it needs little explanation, with things in logical places arranged for easy access. Imagine a child entering your room for the first time; would they know where to go for specific activities? Are passageways between areas clear and unobstructed? Can they easily see how to get to you, their own place and the toilets?

Storage

Keep most items stored at child-level, unless you are trying to prevent the children having access! The range of possibilities for storage items include everything from home-made storage items (wallpaper-covered biscuit tins, hand-sewn wall hangings) to expensive solid wood purpose-made furniture. Overall, clean, bright and cheerful is a good general

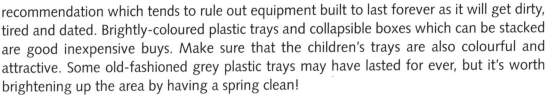

recommendation which tends to rule out equipment built to last forever as it will get dirty, tired and dated. Brightly-coloured plastic trays and collapsible boxes which can be stacked are good inexpensive buys. Make sure that the children's trays are also colourful and attractive. Some old-fashioned grey plastic trays may have lasted for ever, but it's worth brightening up the area by having a spring clean!

If replacement is out of the question, use bright labelling to cheer up trays and drawers. If replacement is in sight, but you need measures to tide you over, cover surfaces in colourful sticky-back plastic which is cheap and cheerful but has a fairly short life. Use lengths of bright curtaining to hide unsightly old shelves and a coat of paint to brighten up an old cupboard door.

If you have the chance to buy new storage units, make sure that you buy something that really is easily movable. Check the castors on the storage units as some are inefficient.

Children's lunch boxes can cause endless trouble so think about a suitable storage option, remembering not to store them near radiators or out of sight.

Labelling

Use labelling in the classroom to help the children identify their places and belongings, using pictures and words. Ask parents to label all the children's clothes and any items they bring into school before they start. Keep a supply of sticky labels to hand in case things need labelling in school.

Allocate each child with a specific picture and use it wherever it might be useful. Label each new child's drawer and clothes peg with their pictures as well as their names. Use the same picture to identify lunch boxes, lunch places, painting aprons and on the cover of the child's first book. Some teachers find it useful to put a child's early work into one book or folder and obviously a picture will help each child to recognise their own. (Choose the pictures carefully, parents may not appreciate their child being identified by a fat slug or Rottweiler.)

Footprints on the floor or arrows on the wall can be used to direct children to vital areas such as the cloakroom or the toilets.

Organising space

Outdoor play areas, the 'home' corner (whether it is a fast food restaurant or a hospital!) and so on, should all be clearly defined. Try to use some form of demarcation so that areas allocated for specific activities are obvious and movement between them is free and easy.

Large department stores think of their space in terms of streams of movement and you can adopt the same approach in the classroom. Mark off one area from another by clear transit corridors and use storage trolleys and bookcases to block off one area from another, making sure the object does not obscure your sight of the children.

Your preparation of the classroom space will help to support the learning that will take place within it. Research tells us that children prefer tidy, organised classrooms to disorganised ones, so take organisation seriously. Check that children know where to put their finished work, and what to do if they finish a task early.

Spaces set aside for specific work could be simply named by colours. The sand tray could be in the yellow area, the bookcase in the red and so on. Confining activities to areas in this way means that you can, if you wish, organise the children's work on a rotating basis with each group having a chart showing where they should be at any given time.

Writing

Have a writing table with ready access to a range of papers (colours and sizes) and writing implements. Writing opportunities can be built into play activities if you set up an office, a shop, garage or restaurant.

Reading

Apart from signs and labels, you should display at least one illustrated alphabet and lots of posters and notices around the room.

A quiet reading space is a must, with books to browse among and displays to entice the children. Provide beanbags or small chairs to make the area appealing and inviting.

Choose themes for displays in the book corner such as dinosaurs, teddy bears and so on and change them often so they don't become just part of the background but an active part of the classroom.

Taped books are useful additions to the reading corner and you can also involve use of the computer as many modern reading schemes have software packages that are worth evaluating, although some are only on CD-ROM.

Decide where you are going to store or display your reading schemes (many schools seem to have at least three as a basic resource) and reading support materials. Is the reading corner the best place or is there a more central area outside the classroom?

Mathematics

A designated area for mathematics-related items is also a good idea which will enable you to promote mathematics as an exciting activity. Don't overcrowd this, or any other of the designated activity areas, but focus on one or two themes only. Make sure that equipment in constant demand (such as Unifix cubes) is readily accessible in easily stacked storage containers which the children can identify and reach.

Display a number line on the wall but also provide a short number line on every child's desk or table to provide a very useful visual aid while they are working.

Art, craft, design and technology

The area used for art and craft activities can get very messy. Select the materials you wish to form the focus of your work and organise the painting and sticking area so that children can easily get at all the materials they will need. Don't mix all the colours for the children – art is a creative learning activity not to be confused with painting and decorating! Even the reclaimed materials for junk modelling need to be sorted and properly stored or it will forever remain junk. Instead use labelled containers to store the sorted items which have been checked for cleanliness and safety.

Seating and furniture

Decisions over what furniture you have in your room will probably have already been taken and your only choices will relate to placement. If you do have the chance to choose new furniture, don't only look in catalogues, visit other classrooms including in other LEAs if possible.

Arguments rage over classroom seating arrangements, often they are ideological rather than practical. Arrange the furniture to suit the shape of your classroom and the activities and teaching that you propose to provide. You must make sure that the children who, for physical reasons, need to be close to you have been catered for. Check for bad eyesight or

Curriculum planning

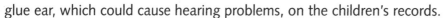

glue ear, which could cause hearing problems, on the children's records.

Children do like to have their own space. Some modern classroom furniture allows children's drawers to be stored under tables which is ideal. However, if you have the old-fashioned sort of furniture where drawers are stacked centrally on a trolley, you must allow for the movement that this requires and adjust your seating arrangements accordingly. Some continental schools have hooks under children's tables where bags can be hung which may be an idea worth consideration.

Consider what you are going to put on the children's tables. How are you going to store pencils, crayons, rulers and erasers? Will you stick a number line on the tables or an alphabet line? Sometimes children want to bring items in from home, while pencils and erasers may be harmless, larger items are best banned because of space restrictions.

Decide which items of furniture and equipment are going to be 'no go' areas for the children, explain this to the children and place the furniture or equipment out of the way.

Try to make your classroom a stimulating space but don't make it over-elaborate or it may become fussy or confusing to the children. Remember the first principle is to make the room logical and approachable, a place where the children quickly feel at home. Be sure that you don't create a classroom that is more suited to your needs than the children's.

Mess

With an enthusiastic group of young children busy at work day after day, it is easy for the room to become untidy. Limit the mess by tidying up at the end of each session and keeping everything in its place.

In addition:
- limit the tools and materials in circulation at any one time;
- scheme and wangle to have a high ratio of adults to children;
- work on easily-cleaned surfaces and floors (outside where possible);
- don't allow unsupervised access to taps and sinks;
- keep practical activities close to taps and sinks and cleaning-up materials;
- always insist that children wear suitable aprons;
- use a teacher's tool tidy box as you move around (to hold essential items such as cloths, sticky tape, scissors, tissues and so on). These can be bought in DIY stores and are particularly useful for classroom assistants who may have to move from area to area or class to class.

Health and safety

Finally, while you are casting your eyes around the room, check for health and safety problems. Are there any obvious hazards? Is the fire exit clear? Do you have an unimpeded view of all the children? Could a child slip out of the room unnoticed?

Time

Teaching in infant classes is rarely delivered in neat lesson-size packages. However if you are going to achieve any kind of balance in the experiences your children receive, or plan for any kind of progression, you will need to decide how you are going to allocate your time. Common sense (and research) tells us that there is a direct connection between the amount of teaching children receive in any subject and their performance in that subject. So, although you may never teach the 'areas of experience' in precisely measured quantities, you should have your 'time budget' in mind when you are planning your curriculum. Bear in mind any special time constraints as well, for example some reception children may only be attending school part-time.

It is useful to note that the DfEE's recommended minimum teaching for infant children is 21 hours per week for a teaching year of 36 weeks. How much time you allocate to areas of the curriculum is not laid down by law, although with the advent of the Literacy and Numeracy Hours this can be said to be changing.

At Key Stage 1 it has been assumed that the core activities of English, mathematics and science will consume more than 60% of the time available. As these subjects overlap considerably at the foundation stage, even this can only be used as a very rough planning guide.

To help your planning, make a timetable which you can follow. It does not need to form a rigid strait-jacket to your work but can show broad allocation of time, perhaps using colour coding. Start by entering in events over which you have no control (hall time, lunch, TV and so on) and activities which are revisited daily such as storytime, registration and 'show and tell' time. Allow time for toilet visits, getting coats, changing for PE and moving from place to place. Research shows that teachers underestimate the time demanded by these non-curricular activities by as much as 20%.

Materials and resources

Inventive and creative reception teachers can and do make use of just about anything in their teaching and are renowned hoarders of odds and ends. The suggestions provided below are ideas to set you thinking and do not represent a comprehensive list.

People

Don't forget to consider people, who can represent a splendid resource. Traditional visitors such as policemen, firemen, lollipop ladies, cooks and cleaners, gardeners and dustmen, vets, nurses, soldiers, librarians or vicars, all provide excellent starting points for learning.

In addition consider asking authors, artists, potters, musicians and parents in to talk about the jobs they do. Try to timetable the term or year's programme as far ahead as possible to fit in with these visitors. Provided they are given adequate notice, most people will be pleased to visit and talk to the children.

In addition to yourself (a key resource!) your classroom assistant or ancillary helper is a very important person in the classroom. Take time to plan how to use her or him and build in time to reflect on the work of the day together.

Audio-visual resources

Some of your audio-visual resources may be stored centrally in the school but, with luck, you will have at least one computer, plus a small tape recorder and a set of headphones with a distribution board for use in your classroom. Store the tapes and disks close to the point of use. Consider night-time security carefully – sets of disks can be as expensive to replace as the hardware and are much more portable.

Assess your available broadcasts and videos well before the start of the year. Choose only a few short appropriate programmes so that you will have time to deal with the content properly.

Materials and activities

A whole range of materials and associated activities will be accommodated in a reception classroom. These will include everyday materials such as pencils, scissors and glue sticks as well as more specific items for topic work. Your day-to-day material requirements will be similar to most other infant classrooms but in addition should include large play equipment especially if most of your children are young four-year-olds. Ideally an outside play area linked to the classroom should be available. The broad areas of provision are:

- sand play;
- water play;
- imaginative play (home corner/hospital/burger bar/shop/boat and so on);
- construction equipment (be selective and allow for progression);
- painting easels and paint;
- tactile activities (play dough/clay/cooking materials);
- creative work (sticking, cutting, fixing, building);
- number corner;
- writing corner (provide different coloured paper and choice of writing tools);
- computer activity (using Concept Keyboard, Pip or Roamer);
- tinkering table (choice of objects to handle and discuss on a theme);
- reading corner;
- music corner;
- interactive displays (pictures or objects linked to tasks).
    Check your activity lists and curriculum plans to ascertain other specific requirements.

Plans and schemes

There is no single best way to plan your year's work and you may, in any case, find that a planning structure and timetable is imposed upon you. One widely accepted approach is to think in terms of long, medium and short-term plans. The long-term (yearly) scheme of things will broadly be dictated by your school schemes and guidelines, medium (termly) and short-term (week-to-week) planning may be almost entirely up to you.

Most observers of recent educational trends are agreed that there has been too much paperwork generated in schools, so keep planning and record sheets to the minimum and keep it simple. An ordinary notebook serves as an excellent daily planning book or diary in which you can record work intentions as well as learning issues or behaviour problems.

However, if you feel that a given structure suits you better than a blank sheet, a number of commercial products are now available such as *The Primary School Diary*, Educational Planning Books, PO Box 63, Hathersage, Hope Valley, S32 1DJ. Telephone: 01433 651010.

Baseline assessment

From September 1998 all primary schools are required by law to use an accredited baseline assessment scheme to assess children within seven weeks of admission to primary school (usually in reception class, but occasionally Year 1). The Qualifications and Curriculum Authority (QCA), is responsible for accrediting and setting guidelines for the baseline assessment scheme which will be used later as a measure in value-added assessments of school performance. Contact the QCA for a list of accredited scheme providers and the latest information.

English
including Literacy Hour

One of the most challenging aspects of the reception teacher's job is to provide an atmosphere in which children feel secure enough to use the language that they already have, and inspired enough to engage in activities which will help to extend this language further.

Getting to know what children can already do in their speaking, listening, reading and writing is therefore essential. It is important to appreciate the impressive abilities which children bring to school with them, and not to underestimate them.

School is a daunting new territory for most children of this age, and it is easy to mistake the shy child's reticence for a lack of language ability. Many children come to school using language varieties that differ from your own, and it is also easy to confuse such language diversity with language deficiency. Communication with parents about these and other matters is vital.

In addition to your input in school, children are exposed to language experiences of all kinds at home. Some of these experiences may not necessarily concur with what you are trying to establish at school, particularly in the case of literacy. For example, parents may discourage their children from using pictures in reading books to make guesses at words because 'guessing is cheating'. Children who go to Saturday classes to learn the script of their community language may be taught that meticulous calligraphy is vital, and so may feel reluctant to engage in free writing at school. Similarly, children whose parents or older siblings tell them that writing requires accurate spelling may go through agonies when a teacher, conducting a writers' workshop session, tells them to 'spell it like you think it should be spelled'.

All of these issues need to be talked over with parents, and workable compromises established which take into account the beliefs and anxieties of both families and professional

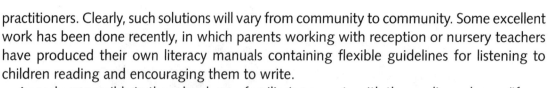

practitioners. Clearly, such solutions will vary from community to community. Some excellent work has been done recently, in which parents working with reception or nursery teachers have produced their own literacy manuals containing flexible guidelines for listening to children reading and encouraging them to write.

As early as possible in the school year, familiarise parents with the reading scheme (if one is followed) and any other structured resources that your school uses. This kind of collaboration can help to provide children with regular, progressive experiences of individual reading at school and at home. Take the opportunity to discuss the content of the material, to explain the way in which decisions are made about placing a child at a certain level and the gradient of challenge that it provides, together with an agreed system for monitoring each child's progress and communicating problems and suggestions.

Parents often express concern that their children don't change their books often enough, or that they bring home books that are too hard or too easy. Pre-empt these worries by providing a thorough explanation of school procedures early in the child's first term.

Literacy Hour

The teaching framework devised by the National Literacy Strategy Framework for Teaching, was the foundation for the Literacy Hour which was introduced into primary schools in September 1998. This one hour every day of dedicated teaching of reading and writing involves a rhythmic transition from whole-class teaching to small-group work and back again.

During this hour, children are engaged in work at whole text level involving comprehension and composition, work at sentence level involving grammar and punctuation, and work at word level involving vocabulary and spelling. Suggestions for the type of work that might be done at each level in the reception class are outlined in the Practical ideas section on page 30.

What should they be able to do?
Key area: Speaking and listening

The language and literacy curriculum for the foundation stage suggests that pupils are given opportunities to speak and listen for different purposes and in different situations including communicating thoughts, ideas and feelings to an adult or their peers. The early learning goals and the objectives for the reception year set out in the National Literacy Strategy are closely linked and provide the basis for planning and assessment.

By the time they have reached the age of five, the vast majority of children have acquired a basic proficiency in the complexities of spoken language. This is a tremendous achievement. Your reception class children can manipulate most of the 44 or so phonemes of English; they have amassed a productive vocabulary well exceeding 3000 words (which may include some surprising words relating to their special interests); they have already mastered the rules by which simple sentences in English are created, and are beginning to come to grips with some of the more complicated processes by which sentences are connected together or embedded within other sentences.

By the end of the school year we can expect that children will have learned many new words about largely school-based pursuits like mathematics, science and PE. Their broadening social world will provide them with lots of opportunities to share new enthusiasms and associated vocabulary with other children, as well as to learn some fresh colloquialisms.

Also, and very significantly, your concern with speaking and listening, reading and writing, will have enabled them to start building up a bank of words with which to talk and think about language itself. They will have been exposed to new contexts for familiar words like *listen*, *question*, and *discuss*, while in the field of literacy words like *word*, *letter*, and *sound* will have been presented to them with extended (and potentially confusing) meanings.

Reception children can use spoken language to initiate conversation, express their needs and feelings, relate their experiences, and to ask and answer questions. They show a readiness to play with language, delighting in the recitation of poems, nursery rhymes, jingles and songs, and the retelling of familiar stories. Some of them will be spontaneously experimenting with language, rolling favourite words on their tongues, or chanting doublets and couplets picked out from conversations, from TV or from stories.

Pronunciation

In pronunciation, most five-year-olds are able to make comprehensible approximations to the 20 or so vowels and 24 or so consonants of spoken English. Less frequent consonants, such as the *dg-* sound in judge and the *zh-* sound in pleasure, might not yet have 'arrived' in the speech of all children. Many children will make swaps between similar sounds. For example, the sound *th-* as in *thread*, is frequently pronounced *f-*, a sound which most children learn earlier. Similarly, the initial or medial *r-* sound in words like *red* and *merry* is often pronounced as a *w-*. Consonant clusters, particularly triple ones such as *str-* and *spl-* may still be presenting difficulties to some children, and it is quite common for them to simplify such clusters to single sounds – *drink*, for example, often comes out as *jink*.

These substitutions are a natural aspect of speech development, and in the vast majority of cases they will vanish as children acquire the very fine control over articulation that such distinctions demand. There is definitely no need to waste your time and to embarrass the children by engaging in futile elocution activities!

Grammatical structure

The grammatical expertise of five-year-olds is perhaps their most impressive achievement. It is important to be clear about what is meant by grammar here. It is not the conformity of children's speech to formal standard English, still less their ability to allocate words to parts of speech categories. Grammar here is seen as the ability to combine words into comprehensible utterances according to intuitively understood rules. This sample of the speech of a typical five-year-old illustrates this.

Yvonne is recalling events from a recent seaside holiday:

that bubbly sea kept running after me and I keeped running quick and I runned up to Anita and she dropped her ice cream because I runned into her and I got wet as anything.

Although this sample clearly originates from a child, the *patterns* by which the words are combined into sentences are similar to those that adult English speakers would use, while retelling a personal experience to a friend. The typical structure of Yvonne's sentences consists of a subject and verb followed by either an object (she dropped her ice cream), a complement (I got wet) or an adverbial (I keeped running quick). *And* is the most common connective between this chain of sentences, its repetitive use enabling the child to pace the narration by combining short, sharp, event reports into a rhythmic story. The use of *because* indicates that other possibilities are present in her repertoire. In fact, our typical five-year-old is capable of supplementing *and* with a whole range of connectives: time indicators like *when, before* and *after*, causal links like *so* and *because*, contrast and alternative words like *but* and *or* and the conditional *if* in such sentences as *If you give it me I won't tell.*

It is important to note that these terms are relatively recent arrivals in the speech of five-year-olds, and that their usage may be limited and somewhat erratic. For example, the ordering of elements in a complex sentence might get a bit mixed up, as in *My baby's hungry because he's crying.* Similar considerations apply to a range of grammatical items, including prepositions, adverbials and tag questions. Patterns like *We went at the shops* are common, as are such confusions as *I like lemon lollies most the bestest, I got two of them, didn't they?* and *Lisa's my very friend and Anna's my another very friend.*

There are three main points to make about such constructions:
- the first is that they are not random errors, but inventive attempts to master new aspects of syntax, and should be seen as signs of growth, rather than as errors;
- the second point is that they are hardly surprising, given the complicated rules that children have to learn;
- the third and most important point is that the child's inventive exploration of these forms rarely leads to serious misunderstanding, (a strategy for dealing with them is under 'recasting' on page 31).

Returning to Yvonne's speech sample, there are further examples of the type of inventive exploration mentioned above. The use of the adjective 'bubbly' is an interesting and effective poetic expansion of the first subject, and a rudimentary simile appears in her final utterance. The use of over-generalisations of the past tense *-ed* rule in words like *keeped* and *runned*

is typical of the speech of five-year-olds, as is the occurrence very nearby of the correct form, showing the transitional state of her language.

It is interesting that the direction of this transition could be either way. Yvonne could be growing out of the use of *keeped* in favour of *kept*, or she could be temporarily favouring *keeped* over the irregular *kept*. Many children begin by picking up the correct past tense forms of irregular verbs like *sat, thought* and *stood*, then, when they become aware that these things are governed by rules, they apply the rules meticulously and start saying *sitted, thinked* and *standed*. This is a very common adjustment to the complexities of English grammar, which many children are beginning to sort out by the end of the reception year.

Again, explicit correction of such transitional phenomena is unlikely to be worth the time spent on it, and risks disrupting the fruitful flow of conversation between adult and child.

Retelling stories

Recounting personal experiences in the classroom will give children the opportunity to demonstrate and practise a certain range of grammatical constructions. The chance to retell and act out stories will vastly expand this range. When a child is retelling a story, there is an often startling expansion in the variety of vocabulary that is used, the complexity of the sentences, and the control over such aspects of syntax as tense. Also, the child's intonation will frequently assume the more ritualistic rhythms of a literary recitation. Children whose speech in naturalistic settings is terse may reveal a submerged capacity for more elaborate and vivid expression. It is as if the story or role play provides a scaffold from which the child can climb into branches of the language tree that are less accessible in spontaneous conversation. Your job is to provide a full range of scaffolding.

This ability to shift the content of speech according to the audience and situation indicates the child's growing pragmatic awareness. Compared to adults, most five-year-olds are relatively unrestrained in their speech, (a quality which can sometimes cause their parents embarrassment). However, they do show signs that they are aware of the ways in which language can be adjusted in accordance with purpose and audience. A five-year-old looking after a doll in the home corner will incorporate into her speech the repetitions, nonsense words and sing-song cadences typical of an adult carer talking to a baby. A child pretending to be a teacher will often adopt an ogre-like manner (which seems to owe more to folklore stereotypes than to real experience).

In spite of this apparent versatility, some finer points of classroom pragmatics still need to be learned. Incongruous expressions like *Please miss, can I go for a pee,* are not uncommon during the child's first days in the reception class, nor should you be surprised if a child responds to a question like *Would you like to give Andrea a turn on the computer now?* with a straightforward *No*. 'Polite' forms of adult discourse, in which commands are disguised as questions or statements are not as transparent to five-year-olds as they are to older children, and their use may need to be preceded by less ambiguous expressions.

Five-year-olds are, of course, capable of expressing messages implicitly rather than explicitly, though they do this with less finesse than adults. A child who says *My cold's nearly all over now* may be hinting that she wants to do outdoor PE with the rest of the class. Such tactics may appear a little obvious to adults, but they do reveal that children are acquiring insights into the thinking processes that underlie the exterior forms of speech.

Listening

The extent to which children can be persuaded to conform to the conventions of thoughtful listening by the end of the reception year is particularly difficult to predict. Children who

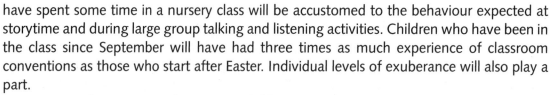

have spent some time in a nursery class will be accustomed to the behaviour expected at storytime and during large group talking and listening activities. Children who have been in the class since September will have had three times as much experience of classroom conventions as those who start after Easter. Individual levels of exuberance will also play a part.

However the majority of reception children will have started to acquire a polite and reflective attitude towards listening to other people speak if they have been:

● given a stimulating variety of stories, poems and information to listen to;
● encouraged to share in the formulation of sensible rules for considerate listening;
● expected to talk about their learning to the class;
● trusted to carry out interesting, collaborative tasks requiring them to follow and convey instructions.

Key area: Literacy

There is likely to be far more variation between the children in your reception class with regard to their reading and writing experience than there is in regard to speaking and listening. In spite of the widespread belief that some children come to school with 'no language', research shows that, though there are significant differences between individuals in speech development, most children *do* participate in stimulating conversations with adults at home. The kinds of competence that have been outlined above are common to most children starting school. Whether or not they display these competencies in the unfamiliar environment of the classroom is a different question.

In the field of literacy, the range of experience that the children will have had will be much wider. Some children who are accustomed to frequent, enjoyable and intensive experience of books and stories at home, will enter your class already able to read simple stories, and to write at least their own names; others, who have had less input of this kind, will possess much more elementary ideas about the forms and functions of print.

No child comes to school *completely* ignorant of written language. Environmental print surrounds children from birth, and in virtually all homes people will be involved in some forms of reading and writing activities, though these might not be of the type that is traditionally regarded as educationally valuable. The summary of points provided here is, therefore, necessarily general, and you should expect a wide range of deviation from the descriptions provided.

Language awareness

Knowing that speech consists of words is a relatively simple form of language awareness that children acquire early. Your reception class children will have quite a robust understanding of this, evident in their ability to choose words for particular purposes, and to answer questions such as, *What's your favourite word?*

The knowledge that spoken words consist of smaller units, is a form of language awareness with important implications for the way in which we teach reading. Knowing that words can be analysed into separate speech sounds or phonemes is, however, a much more sophisticated matter than awareness of whole words, and does not usually begin to develop until children have started to learn to read. This is hardly surprising since, when we listen to somebody talking, we do not attend to individual sounds but to overall meaning. However, there is an aspect of speech/sound awareness that children develop early and take a playful interest in, and that is the way in which words, or more properly syllables, can be separated into initial sounds and rhymes. The technical terms for these units are onset (any part of the syllable that comes before the vowel) and rime (the vowel and anything that follows it).

Thus, though typical five-year-olds will find it very difficult to separate a spoken word like dog into *duh-o-guh*, they will appreciate that dog rhymes with fog, log, hog and bog, and that it shares a beginning sound with words like dish, dirty and dangerous. This again is hardly surprising. The separation of words into individual phonemes is of little intrinsic interest to children, and only becomes important when they are learning to spell.

Alliteration and rhyme however, underlie many of the forms of language that children find fascinating: nursery rhymes, counting out rituals, TV jingles, names like Donald Duck and Mickey Mouse, tongue twisters, and onomatopoeic items like ding-dong and miaow. This sensitivity to alliteration and rhyme suggests that, in the early reading curriculum, rich experience of poetry, song and word play should precede (and form the foundation for) a focus on the sounds of individual letters. The ability to associate sounds and individual letters is important in children's spelling development, but this aspect of awareness seems to develop as an *effect* of learning to read, rather than being a *prerequisite* for it.

Knowing the alphabet

Awareness of the visual aspects of print and how these relate to speech is also a crucial factor in learning to read. Many of the children coming in to reception class will already know how to say the alphabet, though this ability is less informative than an analysis of what each child knows *about* the alphabet. Some of the children will have been taught the alphabet song, which provides a very good start, but does not in itself ensure that they will be able to associate the letters in the song with their printed symbols. Other children will be able to say the names of the letters when shown them, but will be as yet unaware of what sound or sounds they represent in print. Still others will have been taught one sound for each letter (*a, buh*) with or without learning the letter name and will need to learn, as their reading progresses, that letters, particularly vowel letters, can represent a range of sounds.

Sight vocabulary

You can expect that most children will have begun to acquire a sight vocabulary of words that they recognise as whole words, in particular their own names. Five-year-old children are also likely to have a large repertoire of words that they have learned from interaction with print around them. This will include street names and other common signs like *stop*, *sale* and *toilet*, together with the brand names of familiar food products and shops. It is important to stress the word 'interaction' here. Children do not acquire a sight vocabulary simply by being surrounded by frequently-used words; they need to see such words in a variety of contexts, and to have their attention drawn towards the words' distinctive features. Experiments have shown, for example, that a child who says 'Colgate' when asked to read a toothpaste carton may still say 'Colgate' when the word 'Stop' is substituted on the carton in the same font.

Reading

So far, we have dealt only with the bits and pieces of literacy: the sub-units of spoken and written language. What is much more important is the larger picture without which such sub-units are meaningless. What does the typical five-year-old know about 'real' reading?

Plenty! Children at play in the simulation areas of a nursery or reception class (home corner, doctor's surgery, corner shop for example) will engage in a wide range of reading and writing behaviour which shows that they understand many of the practical and recreational functions of literacy.

Many five-year-old children will be able to pick up a storybook whose contents they have become familiar with through listening, and 'read' it to you confidently. A smaller number will be able to do the same thing with an unfamiliar book. In the former case, some children will be reading in the conventional sense of looking at printed symbols and saying out loud the words that the author has set down. Others will be reciting a familiar story in the presence of the text, using illustrations and a corpus of known words from the text as supports for memory.

This latter ability is not to be denigrated or seen as 'cheating'. On the contrary, reader-like behaviour, in which children make the first links between stories enjoyed orally and their representations in print, is an absolutely crucial step on the way to fluent reading. What children need, of course, is plenty of interaction in the course of this experience, during which you can point out the more detailed connections between spoken and written language. The most vivid and effective way of familiarising children with these detailed connections between spoken language and print is by involving children in meaningful writing.

As children's experience of reading and writing grows, so too does their sight vocabulary of whole words, and their ability to make links between common sounds and common spelling patterns in these words. This can be encouraged through such activities as collecting rhyming and alliterating words and composing simple sentences, stories and verses with them. Gradually, their awareness of sounds becomes more finely tuned, and the ability to derive separate phonemes from larger units becomes established.

Writing

From the earliest experiences of mark-making, children understand that the activity of writing can leave tangible, 'readable' traces of their presence. Later, they will learn that visual images can be recorded in this way, and later still, spoken words. A crucial breakthrough, that many of your reception class children will have made or be on the brink of making,

occurs when the child learns to write his or her own name. The creation of this personal label makes writing very significant to a child.

From this starting point, your children can go on to find similarities and differences between the cluster of symbols which denote their own names and those which signify other people and other meanings. At this stage, children become fascinated by initial letters and by letter strings in the environment, which correspond to those in familiar names.

Emergent writing

The degree of confidence with which five-year-old children approach writing varies enormously. Some children are happy to extemporise from their limited knowledge, and will cover pages with combinations of letters and letter-like symbols, few of which they will be able to 'read' back. Others will have acquired a more formal, and hence constricting, view of writing. They may have learned to regard 'emergent writing' as 'scribble' and will refuse to write anything unless they are sure that they have got the spelling exactly right.

It is important to try to respect the different personality types among your children and the conceptions of literacy that underlie such diametrically opposite approaches and aim to tailor your teaching accordingly. The children who won't take risks will need to be helped, through shared writing, to create their first texts; children who write without inhibition will need insights into how writing represents speech in a stable and consistent manner.

Spelling

Children who have gained enough confidence to write without close support may be at a pre-communicative or pre-phonetic level in their spelling. In the first case, words will be represented by pictograms and seemingly random letter combinations; in the second, a rudimentary representation of sounds begins to emerge. Initial letters and some consonants may be present, and familiar letter names may be used to represent syllables (for example *hmt dmt* for Humpty Dumpty). The spacing of words may bear more resemblance to the flow of words in speech than in conventional writing.

Conventions such as directionality will take a while to become established, and you might find the horizontal and vertical orientation of children's writing varying from day-to-day or even page-to-page. The shape and size of the letters themselves will also vary a great deal as children explore the boundaries of flexibility. Letters which are topologically similar, such as f and t, or b, p, q and d, may be used interchangeably until these boundaries become established. This may seem bewildering to an adult but, to a child who has learned to call a cup *a cup* regardless of which way the handle is pointing or whether it is upside down or not, this interchangeability makes perfect sense.

By the end of the reception year, the kind of activities described in the next section should have given your children a firm grasp of the directional principles of English print (follow the words from left to right across the page to the end of the line, then start again at the left end of the next line down) and most children should be able to form their letters correctly – most of the time.

You can expect that, after their time in the reception class, most children will have a firm grasp of the one-to-one match between spoken and written words. They should understand that writing represents language in a stable way, so that the same book always tells the same story, the same caption always delivers the same message. They should be capable, with support, of writing down and reading back simple personal statements. While correct spellings will be the exception rather than the rule, children should be beginning to show awareness of how letter strings represent sounds.

Practical ideas

Developing key areas

Speaking and listening

Open-ended questions

Five-year-old children need plenty of experience both with conversation adjusted to their particular level and with more general talk which places more demands on their ability to listen, comprehend and clarify their own and other people's utterances. The talk that you engage in with the whole class, or with groups, at storytime, when talking about routine procedures, when planning the day's work and play or when introducing new areas of the curriculum, are all examples of general talk. More finely-tuned talk requires individual or small group conversations which will be impossible without the involvement of parents, older children and NTAs in the classroom, working alongside children as they engage in productive and stimulating activities.

Make sure that your helpers realise the need for using open-ended questions which allow the children some input. They should avoid the type of restrictive question and answer pattern exemplified below:

Child: *I did my picture. Look at my picture.*
Teacher: *Oh, look at Adam's picture. What's your picture about Adam?*
Ch: *A tree. It's...*
T: *What colour are the leaves on Adam's tree? What colour are your leaves Adam?*
Ch: *Green.*
T: *Nice and green. Very good.*

Adam does not get the chance to say what he would like to about his picture because his teacher narrows the conversation to a banal 'testing' question about colour vocabulary.

Adults listening

Interactions between adults and children in the classroom should allow space for children to ask their own questions and to talk extensively about their own concerns and discoveries. They should not comprise simply filling in the slots between the adult questions and adult feedback to the child's answers. The emphasis should be on helpers collaborating with children in hands-on activity, sharing their own perceptions of practical tasks (rather than quizzing the children), offering anecdotes, demonstrating techniques, clarifying

misunderstandings and above all perhaps, simply *listening*.

The ability to ration one's own talk, in order to allow space for the children, is an important one for both teachers and helpers to develop. Sometimes adults working alongside children might consider imposing a 'speak when you're spoken to' rule upon themselves!

Recasting

When listening to children talk it is important to focus on and respond to the intended *meaning*, rather than insisting on the child producing the correct *form* before the conversation can continue. Such an insistence is likely to be frustrating and demotivating for the child, and in some cases can lead to a downward spiral of incommunicativeness. Gently probe unclear utterances with questions related to the possible meanings of the utterance and, when the child's intention is clear, incorporate a model of the correct form into your response. This process is known as *recasting*, and is an effective way of maintaining communication while helping children towards more mature constructions.

Content

What should the *content* of the talk curriculum for the reception class include? One of your most important jobs is to get the children to talk about themselves through daily discussions (which might be linked to shared writing), in which children talk about their families, their homes, their favourite interests and foods, their pets and toys, provide obvious starting points.

● Sharing favourite stories, songs and rhymes from home is also an important opportunity to encourage children to contribute. In addition, ask children to contribute to a regular forum based on 'funny things I hear at home' or 'things that annoy me' or 'interesting things I've found' which can be another very effective means of encouraging talk.

Talking about new experiences

Children also need to use talk as a bridge towards novel experiences. Hands-on exploration of materials that may not be available at home, such as clay, paint, fabric and construction materials can provide an enjoyable stimulant for such talk.

Give these experiences some direction by

setting the children fairly open-ended tasks to talk through: *Work together to make the tallest building you can with the Sticklebricks, then make the longest. Use the clay to make a model of your friend. Draw a creature that nobody has ever seen before. Paint what you think you'll look like when you're as old as me.*

Talking about different subjects

Use the full range of subject areas to contribute to the extension of the children's oral repertoire. Here is a brief checklist of some of the opportunities which could encourage talk:

▶ listening to unfamiliar pieces of music;
▶ looking at objects through microscopes and telescopes;
▶ caring for classroom pets;
▶ examining mystery objects, including historical artefacts, and speculating about their uses and origins;
▶ looking at works of art from a range of cultures and periods;
▶ preparing simple but unfamiliar recipes;
▶ using construction materials to make toys and games from other cultures;
▶ making and playing with simple puppets and puppet theatres;
▶ setting-up a small area in which adults and children display 'curiosity' pictures, which might be anything from satellite pictures to photo-micrographs.

Listening games

Listening should be encouraged as an integral part of activities throughout the day, particularly by giving children jobs which require them to act upon spoken instructions. In addition, there are a variety of specific games which you can play with children (such as 'Chinese whispers') to encourage careful listening.

Other ideas include:
● **Noticing nonsense** – Read or tell an account of an everyday event inserting ludicrously impossible features at suitable intervals. The children must listen for these, interrupting the story when they hear them, and suggesting amendments.

Yesterday I was waiting for the bus when a chocolate car went past. When the bus arrived, the skeleton who was driving it asked me ...

A variation is to read a description of a familiar animal or object, inserting silly anomalies.

english

●	**Spoonerisms** – Read a story and transpose parts of selected words so they are spoonerised. The children should listen for these and interrupt and correct: *Goldilocks saw a mysterious little house so she decided to take a wook through the lindow...*

●	**What am I ?** – Give each child a picture of an easily recognisable animal, tool or person. Ask the children to take it in turns to say three things about their object, without actually naming it. Encourage the other children to listen, ask for further information, and then try to guess what the object is.

Storytime

Some of the richest opportunities for talking and listening occur in the field of literacy. Traditional tales from a range of cultures, fantasy stories involving magic and talking animals, stories about the remote past and the future will all help to widen children's linguistic and imaginative horizons.

Storytime should be a daily and sacrosanct occasion, in which you both read and *tell* stories and children learn to listen for increasing periods. Spend little time questioning the children about what happened in the stories, but encourage them to speculate about what might happen next. Make time as well for the children to tell their own stories, or to retell ones that they have heard from other sources.

Daily involvement in listening to and telling stories is probably the best foundation for the development of reading and writing skills.

Parents and literacy

Parental support is an essential foundation for developing literacy in the classroom. As a reception class teacher, you are in a good position to involve parents in helping to build bridges between the types of literacy experience that have been encountered at home, and those at school.

The vast majority of children will have had *some* kinds of such experience before they arrive in your classroom. Even if this has not involved close encounters with print, it is likely that they will have been told stories, joined in songs and rhymes with their carers and seen adults reading the paper, checking a TV schedule, filling in forms or doing word games.

Literacy Hour

The following suggestions provide ideas for the type of work that might be done at whole text, sentence and word level in the reception class.

Work at text level

This is the matrix for everything that comes after it. Enjoyable experience of well-written stories, poems and items of non-fiction is what gives shape and significance to the activities with smaller units such as sentences, words and letters and, if this is neglected, no amount of drilling in isolated word lists or spelling rules will make the child into a reader who enjoys reading or a writer who sees the point of writing.

Shared reading – Big Books

The best way to demonstrate the purposefulness of literacy is through shared book experiences, during which groups of children or whole classes share in the reading and writing of enlarged texts.

Many commercial publishers now produce a wide range of Big Books which are suitable for reception class children, providing enlarged versions of popular titles which can be shared with groups of children. Choral reading of a variety of such texts should be a daily activity.

Select texts whose content and complexity is matched to the interests and the memory span of your children. (Remember that the objective here is not rote memorisation, but the ability to 'recite' in the presence of a text which has previously been shared, discussed and enjoyed.)

Accompany the reading by prediction and discussion of content, and follow it up by activities which focus on word level, such as:

▶	asking children to identify key words in the text;

▶	finding words which begin with a particular letter, or which contain a particular letter string ;

▶	masking words and asking children to use the context of the surrounding words to identify what has been hidden. This elementary form of cloze is a good way of showing children that the meaning of the whole text and the grammatical part of the sentence in which an unfamiliar word is encountered can help them to work out the identity of that word;

▶	using a sliding mask to disclose a word letter-by-letter in order to focus on the links between sound/spelling.

Information technology

Familiar texts on CD can also provide many of the advantages of 'big book' experience in the more intimate context of two children sharing a computer screen. Animated illustrations provide vivid accompaniments to the written story and the words themselves can be highlighted as they are read aloud, thus providing an integrated demonstration of the sound, spelling and meaning of the printed word.

Shared writing – Big Books

Create your own Big Books through shared writing, when you or another helper act as scribe to the children's dictation. This is an excellent way of broadening your reading resources while at

to develop a sense of ownership and pride in their work as well as developing their knowledge about language.

More shared writing

Though stories are the most obvious kind of shared writing, there are other possibilities:
▶ instructions for looking after classroom pets;
▶ discoveries about numbers;
▶ accounts of visits, outings, assemblies and other important events;
▶ safety rules and guidelines for behaviour;
▶ recipes and other types of instructional text;
▶ poems, riddles, jokes and tongue twisters;
▶ letters to parents and other members of the school community;

the same time providing a purposeful context for the demonstration of a whole spectrum of writing skills: the sequencing of events in a story, selection of appropriate vocabulary, sound-to-spelling correspondences, placement of punctuation marks and (after the first draft has been completed), editing and proof-reading.

Two of the main objectives of this activity are to demonstrate the links between talking and writing, and to give children a sense of ownership over their reading materials, and so it is important that the child's exact words are written down. Whether or not they are changed in the final version of the shared writing will depend on discussions with the children (and on the kind of policy compromises with parents mentioned in the introduction). This kind of discussion about editing provides ideal opportunities for children

▶ a class diary focused on a particular project (such as growing things, counting down to preparations for a Christmas production, a school trip or outing).

Guidelines for spellers

Many children will be inspired to want to write independently, or with partners, following the demonstrations provided by shared writing. Those children who are ready for this can do so during the group phase of your lesson, while you work with less confident children.

Set clear guidelines for what would-be independent writers should do if they get into trouble with spelling. For example, some teachers encourage children to attempt the first letter or blend, then to put a line so that the word can be returned to when help is available.

Work at sentence level

These activities are all based on language generated by the children themselves in the course of reading or helping to compose whole texts. They are all designed to involve children in thinking about the sequencing of words within sentences.

The ideal teaching unit for the activities described here is small groups. Work produced by these groups can then be shared by the whole class.

In the reception class, the only punctuation you need to introduce is the full stop, though you can demonstrate the use of other marks if the children's responses show a real need for them. The grammatical terminology used here in describing the activities is for your own consumption. There is no need to avoid such words when doing the work with children, but trying to get five-year-olds to sort words into such categories is thoroughly inappropriate.

Introduce some of these ideas, keeping their use short, frequent and playful.

● Divide texts produced by shared writing into separate sentences for the children to shuffle and reconstruct. Numbered steps in instructional texts such as recipes are a good starting point.

● Cut up sentences into phrase groups which you reassemble one at a time, with the children identifying which word group should come next. Repeat this process with individual words.

● Present sentences with a selected word missing. The children have to use the syntax and the residual meaning of the sentence to suggest substitutions. This helps them to see how thinking about context can help them identify unfamiliar words when they are reading their own books.

● Select particular verbs and nouns and substitute other possibilities for them. Ask the children to decide whether or not the resulting sentence continues to make sense.

● Ask the children to extend sentences using connectives like *and, but, because.*

● They can compose alliterative sentences in which as many words as possible begin with the same letter or blend.

● Create well-supported opportunities around the class for children to take turns at writing a simple sentence on a daily basis. For example, providing a weather chart with stem sentences relating to temperature, wind and rainfall.

● Encourage children to give oral and then written completions to prompt sentences like *I get annoyed when ...*, *If I was Head of this school I would ...* , *My favourite meal is ...*

● Invite children to use their knowledge of story to fill in blank speech bubbles in cartoons based on familiar stories.

Work at word level

Word level activities provide a link between the reading of whole texts and the teaching of letter-sound relationships (phonics). The latter should involve a close integration of attention to both the sounds of spoken words and the visual patterns of their spellings. Many of the activities outlined below might grow out of work with whole texts, encountered orally or through reading, but there is no need to limit children's exploration of phonics purely to words that they come across while reading whole texts.

● Hold frequent games and recitations of rhyming, alliterative and onomatopoeic songs, stories and poems with the children. Make a display which highlights initial letters and rhymes. Traditional songs and nursery rhymes (such as 'Old Macdonald' and 'Jack and Jill') are good sources.

● Play games in which children brainstorm as many words as they can beginning with particular onsets or ending in particular rimes. Adapt 'I Spy' for this. Show, through shared writing, the visual similarities between these words (avoiding those with variable sound/spelling patterns) then show the children how to generate new words by substituting new onsets or new rimes.

● Play odd-one-out activities both orally and in writing to highlight both sounds and spelling of onsets and rimes. For example: *quack, rack, sick, sack.*

● Ask children which words *they* want to learn to write. Provide the words on cards, to build into a personal vocabulary bank and use small shoe boxes (which the children can decorate) to store them. Use these words for text-building activities (such as making sentences and stories) and for activities which focus on sounds and letter patterns.

● Make a big alphabet frieze with capital and small letters and with space for pictures to be added. Let the children find and cut out pictures for each letter and then stick them in the right places. (*Who can find a picture for 'Y'?*).

● Compose orally and then record in writing, a variety of class alphabets: an alphabet of names, of real and imaginary animals, of favourite foods, of places, of books and story characters. Display the results as zigzag books or friezes.

● Include vocabulary lists of relevant words in wall displays about topics on which you are currently working.

● Display frequently-used vocabulary in alphabetical order on a chart which children can help each other to use when they are writing independently.

● Give children frequent, diversified opportunities to play with letters (magnetic ones are ideal), shuffling and sequencing them. One very rewarding activity is to give each child in a group the letters of their own name. A helper can then encourage them to make comparisons and contrasts, to swap, substitute and pool letters, to compose nonsense words and real words using the letters.

Handwriting

Handwriting activities should also start with the child's own name and other personally significant words, though many schools prefer a more structured approach based on a published scheme. In any case, the child's name provides an ideal context for learning the relationship between upper and lower case letters.

● Develop awareness of the features which distinguish letters by: encouraging children to look at similarities and differences between common words and those in their personal vocabulary collection; talking about features of environmental print; seeking out particular letters in that print. Computer programs are also available in which children can watch animated alphabets demonstrating the shape, formation and sound values of given letters.

● Enhance correct letter formation through activities in which children follow dot-to-dot patterns for given letters to trace over words you have written. Drawing letters in the air and tracing them onto textured surfaces can also help. Make the repetition needed for mastery over letter shapes more interesting by asking the children to use repeated letter patterns to decorate the borders of their written work.

● Remember that handwriting is a graphic art as well as a linguistic one. For this reason any activity that develops dexterity and aesthetic awareness such as drawing, modelling and the use of hand tools is likely to be beneficial to handwriting skills.

 Ideas bank

Nursery rhymes

Recite rhymes with the children. Pause at the rhyming word, cueing the children to provide it.

● Make up nursery rhymes and repeat this process, so that children are participating in the *composition* process.

● Ring the changes on known nursery rhymes, substituting both elements that maintain the original rhyme and others that change it.

● Ask children to learn a new (old) nursery rhyme from an older family member.

● Base an assembly on the performance of some nursery rhymes, including those collected from the children's family research. Invite the children's informants to attend, or even participate in the occasion.

Classroom book factory

Ask helpers to make large quantities of books in a variety of formats, from simple folded and stapled softbacks, through zigzag books and comb bound books, to stitched books with card covers.

Tell children coming in to school on their first day in the reception class that a blank book is waiting for their authorship. Brisk use of shared writing might enable children to take their own book home after only one day at school!

Later, use new books from the classsroom store for a special class activity or display or for independent writing by individual children.

Fifteen-minute interviews

Invite a parent or another member of the school community to give a five-minute talk on any topic appropriate for five-year-olds, then to stay for another ten minutes of children's questions. Afterwards use their contribution as the basis for a variety of art and language work. Finish by using the children's work as the basis for letters to the visitor.

Suggested topics could include: *My first day at school, The naughtiest thing I ever did, The funniest thing that ever happened to me, How to make a ...*

Tape bank

Invite parents to contribute to a bank of taped stories, which the children can listen to while 'reading' the appropriate book.

Choose a popular series such as the Ahlberg's *Happy Families* stories and arrange for a different parent to record each story. Ideally use people with different accents or encourage parents to role play!

Assessment

Speaking and listening

The assessment of speaking and listening is a notoriously problematical area. Establishing just what constitutes skilled use of oral language is extremely difficult to specify. In addition, you cannot assume that children lack a particular skill just because they have not produced evidence of it on the occasions when you have been able to observe.

For example, children who don't listen to a particular story might just be bored by that story, rather than be lacking in 'listening skills', (which are very difficult to identify accurately) since listening depends so much on what interests the individual. Similarly, a child's lack of communication at school might be caused by shyness, language difference or unfamiliarity with school conventions rather than by lack of oral ability.

Keeping records

The problems inherent in assessing speaking and listening demonstrate the need to keep informal but wide-ranging records of each child's speaking and listening in a variety of contexts and with a variety of partners. They also highlight the need to attend to what the child's family say about his/her speaking and listening outside school.

Many teachers find that the most convenient way of collecting information in this area is to have a notebook with a page or two dedicated to each child. This can be left in a position where incidental observation, including verbatim snippets, can be jotted down by the teacher or a classroom assistant. In order to build up a systematic picture, you might focus on a small number of children to observe each day. Over the course of time, these observations can help to inform judgements about how well the children are progressing in such aspects of oral language as the following:

- communicating simple needs;
- participating in the recitation of repetitive patterns from stories and poems;
- responding personally to stories read aloud or shared with an adult during a reading conference;
- awareness of rhyme and alliteration;
- listening to, conveying and acting upon instructions;
- listening and responding to other children in group work;
- relating personal experiences and sharing personal interests, telling and retelling stories;
- asking questions about things that are difficult, interesting or puzzling.

Literacy
Reading conference

As a reception class teacher, one of your most important tasks is to assess individual children's literacy abilities during their first weeks in school. Talking to parents is essential here, but it is equally essential to organise a reading conference with each new child as soon as possible after they start in your class. Try to make this as relaxed an occasion as possible. Physical comfort is essential (most good readers associate their earliest memories of reading with

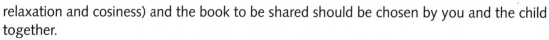

relaxation and cosiness) and the book to be shared should be chosen by you and the child together.

Aim to spend some of this time reading *with* the child, some of it listening *to* the child reading, and the rest of it talking about that particular book and about reading in general. (Of course, with many five-year-olds, the second of these phases might consist of the child simply reciting a line or two based on shared reading.) As the child reads, make notes about the strategies being used (simple memorisation, attention to sound-spelling relationships, word length, pictures, context), and try to assess through discussion the child's appreciation and comprehension of the text.

The individual reading 'conference' in which a child and teacher share a book together, is an essential part of teaching and diagnostic assessment. The observations made during this time will enable you to make decisions about what instruction to give the child during the teaching time outlined above and what level and type of book the child should read next.

Recording systems

After the initial conference, inexperienced readers like your five-year-olds should read with you, or with another competent reader, at least two or three times a week. Published recording systems such as the *Primary Language Record* (CLPE, 1988) and *Progress in English* (RALIC, 1995) provide useful formats and detailed guidelines for the systematic reporting and interpretation of the information you gain in listening to the children read. Remember that this is a time not just for assessment, but for teaching children to apply what they have learned about context clues and sound/spelling relationships to the reading of their own books. It is also a time in which you can show them how to respond critically.

Reading diaries

The reading conference is probably your richest source of data on the child's reading progress, but a fuller picture should also include elements such as reading diaries. In these parents and teachers can write to each other about what the child is reading and the reading strategies used. They can include a record of the types of book and other material that the child has enjoyed, and information on the child's own view of her/himself as a reader.

Tick list records

In addition to the information gleaned on the child as a 'holistic' reader, many reception class teachers also like to keep tick-list type records in which the child's growing familiarity with particular phonic elements and items of sight vocabulary are monitored.

Clearly, a cumulative record of the child's alphabetical knowledge (comprising the names, sounds and formation of each letter) could be kept in this way, as could a record of the child's ability to recognise items from a list of high frequency words. (The National Literacy Strategy *Framework for Teaching* provides suggested word lists for each age group.)

Writing records

Much of what has been said about the assessment of reading, also applies to writing. Observing children's writing and talking to them about their work should help you to construct a picture of their skills and attitudes.

Dated samples of writing of various types can be supported by observational notes about the children's approach to the task, the level of help that they needed and their own reflections on their work.

Maths
including Numeracy Hour

Teaching and learning opportunities provided in the reception class will lay the mathematical foundations on which all other pure mathematics (mathematical knowledge, skills and understanding) and applied mathematics (real-life, problem-solving investigations) are built in later years.

These experiences should allow young children to begin to develop a firm understanding of mathematical concepts and to recognise the connections between:

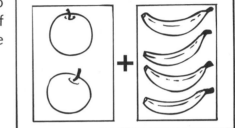

- mathematical symbols – '+', '=' signs;
- mathematical language – plus, add, equals;
- pictures;
- concrete situations – (*Two apples add four bananas. How many pieces of fruit altogether?*)

Children should be familiar and successful with the materials, language and activities for each learning objective before starting activities related to the next objective. However, mathematics is not a fixed, linear, hierarchical discipline: it is cumulative rather than sequential. Although the learning objectives in this chapter show a step-by-step sequence, the way you use them will depend upon the needs, strengths and abilities of individual children.

Language

Children need to experience mathematics in a rich oral environment, for it is through language that they make meaning out of their experiences. When you ask children to talk about what they are doing and thinking in mathematics, they not only show you how much they understand but they also clarify and develop their own understanding.

While you need to accept children's early mathematical vocabulary, you should help them to develop more formal mathematical language as it is required. For example, when learning about addition, children first use terms such as *and*, *altogether*, and *how many*, however, while you are talking to them you can informally use words such as *add*, *plus* and *equals*.

You need to be continually asking questions that will help children:
- Make connections in mathematics – the link between the teaching and learning objective currently being taught and that of previous objectives taught: *Do you remember our work on 2D shapes last week? Does that help you to answer the question?*
- Develop a greater understanding of the learning objective – the link between the teaching and learning objective and the various mathematical activities: *What have you learned from the game you have just played?*
- Make new discoveries in mathematics – bring to children's attention a new concept that is evident from the current teaching and learning objective: *What have you done so far?*

● Apply their mathematical knowledge to other contexts – money, shape, measures, other problems: *If we know that 3 + 2 = 5, what do you think that 3p + 2p equals?*

Children new to English

You may have children in your class for whom English is a second or other language and the ability of these children to communicate in English will vary considerably. This makes your job of ascertaining where they are in their mathematical understanding and where to take them forward all the more difficult. ESOL children need to be exposed to the English mathematical vocabulary and symbols as soon as possible. However, they first need to be able to make the connection between both the written and spoken mathematical language and symbols of their mother tongue and their English equivalents. You may find there are mathematical charts in community languages available in your area. If not, enlist the help of parents or older children who speak the language you need, to prepare charts with you. For example:

Unlike Modern Arabic many languages do use the same symbols as English.

You, or a helper can 'read' the chart with children as they count in their mother tongue and you count in English. Pair ESOL children with English-speaking children who have a good grasp of counting and they can teach each other to count in their mother tongues.

Estimation and approximation

Provide your children with plenty of opportunities to estimate a rough answer to a problem, and approximate the range an answer is likely to occur within. This will help them to develop a 'feel' for numbers and assess whether an answer is reasonable or not. These skills also play an important role in their ability to measure with understanding. Real-life activities such as cooking, sewing and building will also help to develop their estimation and approximation skills.

Linking concrete apparatus and mental mathematics

In the reception class it is imperative that children's first experiences of the world of mathematics are with concrete materials and familiar real-life objects. As they work with these, they can see and touch the mathematics they are engaging in.

There does, however, come a time when children are ready to move away from manipulating concrete apparatus and can begin to internalise their understanding. This internalisation of the mathematics can be thought of as the initial stage of 'mental mathematics'.

Unfortunately, children don't give off a signal when this 'internalisation' has occurred! So it is difficult to know precisely when the need for concrete apparatus has passed. It is only through observation as well as questions and discussions with the children that you can begin to ascertain whether they are ready to work without concrete apparatus.

For example: *You have just shown me that if you have three blocks and you add another three blocks, you will have six blocks altogether. Let's put the blocks away. Can you tell me what is three add four?*

There will, however, be times when children will need to return to using concrete apparatus and such materials should always be available for them to use whenever they want them.

Practical experiences

Practical learning situations, where children use concrete apparatus in real-life problem-solving investigations, often require a considerable amount of time to organise. However, provided that practical work is properly structured, with clear learning objectives, and is followed up by appropriate questions and group discussions, it is time well spent.

For many young children practical work provides the most effective means of understanding a particular mathematical concept. It enables them to think through the mathematics contained in the situation and develop a greater understanding of the learning objective.

Children's recording

In the reception class the emphasis should be on practical experiences and talking about mathematics. Children should not be required to write or copy mathematical problems. Gradually they will want to record their results and should be encouraged to do so using their own methods of recording. Eventually they will want to use the more conventional recording techniques. This is the time to introduce the standard or formal methods of recording using mathematical signs and symbols, for example: 3 + 4 = 7.

Numeracy Hour

The key objectives in the *National numeracy strategy: Framework for teaching* (NNF) for the reception year are in line with the early learning goals for mathematical development published by QCA.

By the end of the reception year if you have based your teaching on the objectives in the Framework you will have helped to prepare the children for starting the National Curriculum in Year One. In Year One the children will be taking part in daily-dedicated maths lessons of about 45 minutes. During this 'Numeracy hour' at Year One, all the children will be working on mathematics at the same time for the whole period. The mathematics work is focused on specific mathematical concepts and methods.

The approach recommended in the NNF for reception children is based on the typical organisation of a reception class - including the use of stories, rhymes, sand and water play, imaginative play, games and cookery. The NNF suggests that a daily mathematics lesson for reception should take the form of:

Whole class introduction
● Usually involving counting, finger games and number rhymes.

Whole class teaching
● Teaching of the whole class on the day's main maths topic.

Group activities
● Either for the whole class, in groups, simultaneously;
● or through one or more play activities worked on by groups, in turn, during the day and usually supported by an adult.

Plenary
● Whole-class session to consolidate and extend the learning.

What should they be able to do?
First experiences

Before entering the formal world of mathematics, reception children need to have opportunities that will help them to develop a 'readiness' for mathematical learning. These first experiences are essential in developing children's ability to begin to think mathematically and to gain the necessary confidence in mathematics, especially when dealing with the abstract notion of numbers. The first of the activities in each section of the Practical ideas provide this kind of preparation.

The problem of the staggered intake into the reception class at the beginning of the academic year is of particular concern to most reception teachers who wonder: How do I present mathematics to each group of children as they enter the class? What do I do with those children who have been in school longer? What about the children with/without nursery experience?

One organisational method that many teachers employ is to have the children working in groups. The children who are new to the class work with the teacher while she presents a new concept, the children who have been in the class longer, work alone or with a classroom assistant to consolidate previously taught concepts.

Another strategy is to have the entire class together and to re-teach the concept. For those children who are new it will be an introduction to the concept, for those children who have been in the class longer it will be a re-introduction. Many teachers worry unnecessarily about re-introducing concepts to their children. If you re-introduce the learning objective, children are able to gain a greater understanding of it and become more confident about it.

Key area: Using and applying mathematics

When planning for Attainment Target 1 you need to provide children with opportunities to:
● use and apply mathematical knowledge, skills and understanding that have been previously taught and practised and consolidated in problem-solving situations;
● acquire knowledge, skills and understandings through 'real-life', meaningful, problem-solving investigations.

By the end of the year, most children should have had appropriate and sufficient experiences that will help them in the key areas listed below. (The statement 'Children should' refers to the majority of children.)

Making and monitoring decisions to solve problems

Children should be able to:
● select and use materials appropriate for a particular task;
● select and use mathematics appropriate for a particular task;
● plan their work both mentally and using simple diagrams or pictures;
● check their work;
● complete a task.

Developing mathematical language and communication

Children should be able to:
● make sense of a task;
● interpret mathematical information;
● talk about their work using simple language;
● record work simply.

Developing mathematical reasoning

Children should be able to:
● ask simple questions;
● make and test simple predictions and statements;
● make a simple generalisation.

Key area: Number

Early understanding in number is developed through activities and discussions about sorting, classifying and comparing groups of objects.

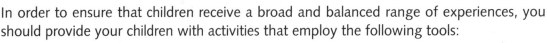

In order to ensure that children receive a broad and balanced range of experiences, you should provide your children with activities that employ the following tools:

- concrete materials;
- mental mathematics;
- paper and pencil;
- information and communication technology.

Mathematics

Place value

Children should to be able to:

- count forwards to 20, and count backwards from 20;
- read, write and order numbers to 20;
- recognise written number names to 10;
- recognise numbers just before and just after numbers 1 to 19;
- count a set of objects to 20;
- make groups of objects to 20;
- compare groups of objects using *more than* and *less than*;
- understand *the empty set* – zero;
- understand one-to-one correspondence;
- sort groups of objects by number;
- match groups of objects with numbers;
- estimate the size of a group of objects;
- recognise ordinal numbers to 3rd.

Money

Children should to be able to:

- understand what money is;
- recognise 1p, 2p, 5p, 10p, 20p coins;
- describe coins;
- match coins;
- classify and sort coins;
- recognise patterns involving money;
- copy, continue and devise patterns involving money;
- use coins in simple contexts.

Methods of computation

Patterns

Children should to be able to:

- recognise patterns involving numbers;
- copy, continue and devise patterns involving numbers.

Addition

Children should to be able to:

- add one more to a given set;
- demonstrate the meaning of addition by joining two sets of objects;
- use concrete materials to add up to 5;
- use the addition + and equals = signs;
- use concrete materials to add two numbers to 10 by combining them;
- use concrete materials to add two numbers to 10 by counting on.

Subtraction

Children should to be able to:
- demonstrate the meaning of subtraction by taking away one object from a set of objects;
- demonstrate the meaning of subtraction by taking away more than one object from a set of objects;
- use concrete materials to subtract up to 5;
- use the subtraction – and equals = signs;
- use concrete materials to subtract two numbers to 10 by taking away.

Solving numerical problems

Children should be able to:
- solve numerical problems involving known addition and subtraction facts in the context of real-life, investigative problems involving:
  - money;
  - length;
  - mass;
  - volume and capacity;
  - time.

Classifying, representing and interpreting data

Children should to be able to:
- sort objects using a given criteria;
- sort objects using more than one given criteria;
- sort and classify objects using own criteria;
- create a Venn diagram;
- create a Carroll diagram;
- record observations using objects or drawings.

Shape, space and measures

Children enter school with a practical understanding of their world gained through their own movement, interaction with others and with everyday objects around them.

Activities involving concrete apparatus provide opportunities for allowing children to develop their spatial and geometric skills, knowledge and understanding.

Measurement using informal units follows the practical experiences of free and structured play. In the reception class, measurement involves comparisons using familiar apparatus and parts of the body.

Patterns and properties of shape

Patterns

Children should be able to:
- experience undirected and directed play involving apparatus that will promote their understanding of patterns;
- recognise patterns;
- copy a pattern using a variety of attributes;
- continue a pattern using a variety of attributes;
- devise a pattern using a variety of attributes;
- make generalisations about patterns;

Mathematics

- make predictions about patterns;
- record observations using own methods.

3D Solids
Children should be able to:
- experience undirected and directed play involving 3D solids;
- recognise 3D solids in the environment;
- build, stack and model 3D solids from the environment;
- match 3D solids;
- sort, compare, classify and describe 3D solids;
- recognise patterns involving 3D solids;
- copy, continue and devise patterns using 3D solids;
- recognise and name a cube.

2D Shapes
Children should be able to:
- experience undirected and directed play involving 2D shapes;
- recognise and name a square, circle, rectangle and triangle;
- recognise 2D shapes in the environment;
- match 2D shapes;
- sort, compare, classify and describe 2D shapes;
- recognise patterns involving 2D shapes;
- copy, continue and devise patterns using 2D shapes.

Position and movement

Position
Children should be able to:
- understand and use simple vocabulary to describe the position of an object in relation to themselves;

- understand and use simple vocabulary to describe the position of an object in relation to other objects;
- describe the position of an object in models, pictures and sketches;
- distinguish left from right.

Movement
Children should be able to:
- participate in movement games and activities;
- follow simple directions;
- give and describe simple directions.

Measures
Length
Children should be able to:
- use materials to make long and short constructions;
- understand the basic language of comparison: long/short, tall/short, near/far;
- compare the length of two objects;

- compare the height of two objects;
- compare the distance between two objects;
- order length, height and distance by direct comparison;
- select objects which are about the same length, height, distance apart as a given object;
- understand conservation of length, height, distance;
- measure length, height, distance using non-standard units.

Mass

Children should be able to:
- push, pull and handle objects in order to become aware of mass;
- understand the basic language of comparison: *lighter than, heavier than*;
- compare the mass of two objects by feel;
- order the mass of objects by direct comparison;
- select objects which have about the same mass as a given object;
- understand conservation of mass.

Volume and capacity

Children should be able to:
- pack, pour and fill containers;
- understand the basic language of comparison: full, half-full, empty;
- compare the capacity of two containers by pouring;
- order the capacity of objects by direct comparison;
- select objects which have about the same capacity as a given object;
- understand conservation of capacity.

Time

Children should be able to:
- understand and use basic language associated with time: *daytime, night-time, yesterday, today, tomorrow, all day, a long while, a little while, morning, afternoon, evening, night, now, later, before, after, week*;
- order events within a day;
- order events over more than one day;
- order events – past, present, future;
- name the days of the week;
- compare the duration of two or three events;
- understand the concept of time passing;
- use non-standard measurements;
- have some understanding of *o'clock* times.

Practical ideas

Classroom organisation

The following practical ideas can be taught in different ways. Nearly all of them can be introduced to the whole class – perhaps with the children sitting round you on the carpet. The children can then continue or complete the activity in groups, either of mixed-ability or like-ability. Offer extension ideas to groups who finish first, ideas for these can be found in the *Variations* of the activities.

Some activities, particularly games, are suitable for children working in pairs and children can work on many of the activities individually.

Making a start

The first activities under each main heading are particularly suitable for introducing the concept.

Progression

Generally speaking there is progression within the group of activities under each main heading, and so you may want to follow the sequence shown. Activities can be adapted, varied or extended to meet the varying needs of your children.

Assessment

Almost all of the activities can be used for some form of assessment. However, activities that have the ○ next to them are particularly suitable for assessment purposes.

Numeracy Hour

Many of the practical ideas which follow in this section are suitable for using in the Numeracy Hour. For example, if you were consolidating children's understanding of addition and introducing the + and = symbols, your Numeracy Hour could follow this pattern:

Whole class introduction and teaching
▶ Which number is one more? (see page 52)

Group activities
▶ Addition feely bag (see page 52).
▶ Use circles for addition (see page 53) with the addition and equals symbol cards.

Plenary
▶ Ask individual children to share with the rest of the class what they have been doing.
▶ Discuss the main teaching points of the lesson.

🔵 Number

Understanding place value

Recite and sing counting and number rhymes with the children. For example: 'Once I caught a fish alive'; 'One man went to mow'.

Conservation activities

🔵 ✪ Conservation of number means understanding that the number of objects in a group remains the same regardless of the arrangement.

For the first arrangement ask: *Are there more cars or boxes?*

For the other arrangements ask: *Are there more cars or boxes now?*

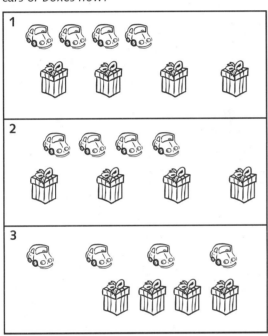

Repeat this at various times with different arrangements of different objects.

🔵 ✪ Arrange two groups of counters/objects. *Which has more? Which has fewer?*

One-to-one correspondence

🔵 ✪ Children match knives and forks; spoons and plates; dolls and chairs and so on:

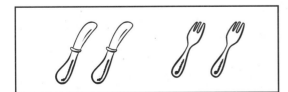

Later, children match objects in a set to cards with number names:

Counting

🔵 Make a book and then a chart about 1, 2, 3, 4, 5 ... Display number, number name and a set of objects representing the number:

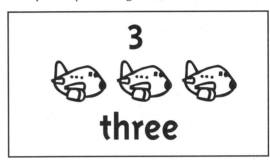

🔵 ✪ When the children are sitting in a circle, get them to count in order with each child saying a number in turn (from 0–20). Then count down from 20 to 0.

Variation: As the count goes round the room, each child has to say the next number using a different voice – softly; loudly; as if they are scared; happy; like a dog, cow; and so on.

🔵 Have an estimation table in the classroom with a variety of things which offer opportunities for estimation (up to ten). *How many cubes in the jar? How many dots on the page?* Ask the children to explain how they got their estimate.

🔵 Have cards marked 0–20 as:

| Numbers | Number names | Number picture cards |

Use the cards as flash cards and ask the children for instant recall as you show them individual cards – start with 0–5 and move on to the higher numbers when they are ready.

Empty set

● Have cards which show all three representations on them:

6

six

Introduce the concept of the 'empty set' by showing cards with 0, zero and no objects. *Why is there no picture on this card?*

Grouping, matching and ordering

● ☼ Ask children to group objects in 5s then 10s leading to 20.

● ☼ Children can order a set of number cards/ number name cards/number picture cards to 5 then to 10 leading to 20.

● ☼ Put 5, then to 10, leading to 20, number cards/number picture cards and/or number name cards in order. Remove a card. *Which number is missing?*

● ☼ Arrange 5 (then 10, then up to 20) number cards/number picture cards and/or number name cards in order, with two cards out of order (for example 1, 2, 4, 3, 5). *Can you rearrange the numbers in the correct order?*

● ☼ Children make a tower of cubes to match each number card to 5 then to 10 leading to 20.

● ☼ Children order a set of number cards with matching groups of objects to 5, then to 10 leading to 20.

Number line

● ☼ Use a number line to 5, then to 10, leading to 20.
1 Point to a number: *What is the number before/ after it?*
2 Point to a number: *What number is one more/ one less?*
3 Point to a number: *Name a number that is greater/less?*
4 Point to two numbers: *Which number is greater/less?*
5 *What number(s) come(s) between (two given numbers)?*
6 Provide a number line with some of the squares blank for the children to fill in.

Number games

● Play attribute games involving numbers: *My secret number is bigger than 10 but smaller than 20.*

● Play 'Guess my number': think of a number and children have to ask questions to try and identify it. *Is it smaller than 10?*

● Dice game: two children throw a dice and choose the matching number card and/or

number name card for the number of dots shown on the dice (1–6).

Variations: 1 Throw two dice and choose the matching number card and/or number name card for the total number of dots (2–12).

2 Throw three dice and choose the matching number card and/or number name card for the total number of dots (3–18).

● Matching game 0–5: working in pairs, children shuffle number cards (0–5), and number name cards (zero–five) together and then play Pelmanism.

Variations: 1 Use number cards and number picture cards.

2 Use number name cards and number picture cards.

3 Repeat for 0–10 and 0–20.

Matching

● ☺ Children can match number cards/number name cards with the total number of dots on a domino:

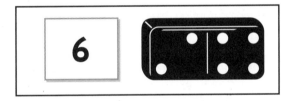

● Match number cards/number picture cards and/or number name cards with numbers on your class number line.

Ordinal numbers

Children will learn ordinal numbers if you use them in daily classroom talk: *Which table will be quiet and tidy first? Oh dear, that's the second time I've found a painting shirt on the floor today. How quickly can you get ready for PE? Kamal's first, Amy's second, Jack's third ... Well done!*

● ☺Ask children to set up a race display with toy cars. Establish and mark the finishing line and give them labels to put beside the cars to show which are 1st, 2nd and 3rd. Later other groups can rearrange the cars and re-position the labels.

Money
Introducing coins

● Talk about shops and the different types of shops. *What do people use to buy things with?*

● Show children a 1p coin, say: *this is a one pence coin*. Write 1p on the board. Repeat for 2p, 5p, 10p, 20p coin. Revise by asking: *What coin is this?* Discuss the size, colour and shape of the coins.

● Children can then: match a collection of 1p, 2p, 5p, 10p, 20p coins; sort coins according to size, colour, shape and value; copy, continue and make patterns using 1p, 2p, 5p, 10p, 20p coins.

● ☺*Sort out this pile of coins. How did you do it?*

● ☺Place 1p, 2p, 5p, 10p and 20p coins in a feely bag. Ask individual children to choose a coin by feel and say what they think it is. They then pull the coin out and see if they were right.

Coin matching game

● Shuffle a range of price cards (for example 3 × 1p, 2p, 5p, 10p, 20p) and spread the cards face up on the table. Put corresponding coins in a bag. The children can take turns to choose a coin from the bag and place it beside the correct price card. If it matches, the player keeps it. If it doesn't match, the player must return the coin to the bag. Game continues until all the coins are used.

The classroom shop

● The children can play 'shops', using price cards (1p, 2p, 5p, 10p, 20p), and purses with coins (1p, 2p, 5p, 10p, 20p) and a collection of shop items (labelled 1p, 2p, 5p, 10p, 20p). One child is the shopkeeper, the other children are shoppers. The shoppers choose an item and offer the correct amount of money. The shopkeeper must check to see that the amount offered is correct before accepting the coin and handing over the purchase. *How much money is there in the till/ in your purse?*

● Children design their own money – invent new designs for all denominations of coins.

Methods of computation
Patterns

● ☺Individual children copy and continue patterns involving numbers to 5, then to 10, leading to 20.

Mathematics

● ☺ Children sort a pack of number cards/number name cards/number picture cards.

● ☺Children make and explain their own number patterns and display them on mobiles around the classroom.

Addition and subtraction

Children should have experiences of addition and subtraction using all of the following:
- real objects (marbles, toys, books);
- mathematics apparatus (counters, cubes, Unifix, Cuisenaire, Dienes);
- numbers (number cards);
- number lines (stick one on every table);
- 0–10 chart.

Development of children's understanding of addition and subtraction should occur as follows:
- you demonstrate;
- children handle the materials, you record;
- children handle the materials, they record.

● Teach them about the commutative aspect of addition: 2 + 3 = 3 + 2. Use interlocking cubes to demonstrate:

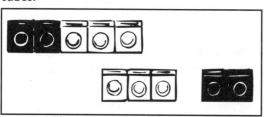

Teach them about the relationship between addition and subtraction, using interlocking cubes:

Give them experiences of calculations involving missing numbers: 2 + 2 = [ ], 2 + [ ] = 5, [ ] – 3 = 2

Show them the patterns in addition and subtraction:

0 + 5 = 5	5 – 0 = 5
1 + 4 = 5	5 – 1 = 4
2 + 3 = 5	5 – 2 = 3
3 + 2 = 5	5 – 3 = 2
4 + 1 = 5	5 – 4 = 1
5 + 0 = 5	5 – 5 = 0

● With number and sign cards, show them how number families work. Number families for 5 are:

0, 5, 5	1, 4, 5	2, 3, 5
0 + 5 = 5	1 + 4 = 5	2 + 3 = 5
5 + 0 = 5	4 + 1 = 5	3 + 2 = 5
5 – 0 = 5	5 – 1 = 4	5 – 2 = 3
5 – 5 = 0	5 – 4 = 1	5 – 3 = 2

As you introduce number facts, make a display/mobile/chart of them.

Addition

Counting on

● ☺ Children count on from any given number to 20: 6, 7, 8, 9,…

● ☺ Display a group of objects. *How many objects would there be if there were one more?* Repeat for different numbers. Extend to 'two more'.

● ☺ Choose either number cards/number picture cards and/or number name cards. Show a card and ask: *Which number is one more?* Repeat for different numbers. Extend to 'two more'.

● ☺ Place five cubes in a feely bag as the children count. Then add another two. *How many are there altogether in the bag?* Repeat using different amounts of cubes.

Addition facts

● Use interlocking cubes for addition facts for 3, 4 and 5.

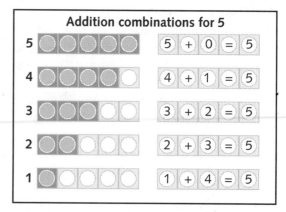

Make rods of connecting cubes using two colours. Show Rod 5. Ask: What is 5 add zero? When they have answered, ask a child to make the number sentence with number cards.
Show Rod 4. Ask: What is 4 add 1?
Pairs of children with appropriate rods, cubes and cards can then build their own addition patterns.

● Using two dice, pairs of children can take turns to throw the dice, add the numbers together and choose the corresponding number card.

Introducing symbols

● Use '+' and '=' symbol cards and 1–6 number cards. A child chooses a number card (4). *Which number is one more than four?* Introduce the + symbol by placing the + card beside the 4 number card and then the 1 number card: 4 + 1. *What is four and one more?* Now introduce the equals sign =: 4 + 1 = . When the answer has been given, place the five: 4 + 1 = 5. Repeat for different numbers. Extend to *two more than*: 4 + 2 = 6.

● Place a number of objects into one circle, and a number of objects into a second circle:

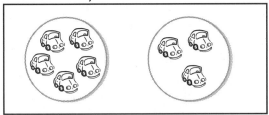

Ask the children to count the number of objects in the first circle, 1, 2, 3, 4, 5.

Introduce the addition (+) sign on a card:

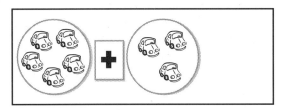

Ask children to continue counting on from the number of objects in the first circle, 1, 2, 3, 4, 5, 6, 7, 8. Introduce the equals = sign on a card:

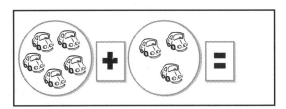

Tell the children that 5 + 3 = 8. Ask a child to choose a card with the number 8 on it and place it next to the equals sign.

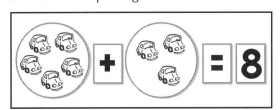

For a class assembly about subtraction use a dais or some benches to make a big 'bed' for ten children to lie on. The class sings 'There were ten in the bed' and the children on the bed act it out. After the song, pairs of children can then say 'That was a song about subtraction. We saw that ten minus one left nine.' Another pair says, 'Nine minus one left eight.' and so on.

Using two sets of 0–5 number cards and + and = symbol cards, children work in pairs. The first child chooses a number card, for example 4, then puts down the + card, the second child chooses another number card, for example 3, and puts down the = sign. Together both children work out the answer.

● ✿ Children make up addition number sentences (using symbols, pictures or apparatus) for 5.

Addition game
● A child rolls a dice and takes the corresponding number of counters. Child throws the dice a second time and takes the number of counters indicated. Child joins both groups of counters together and counts to complete the addition. *Variation*: 1 Child chooses corresponding number cards.
2 Team game: as above, however the first child to get three number cards which will make a row, for example 10, 11, 12, is the winner.

Subtraction
Counting back
● Sing 'Ten green bottles'. Put a row of plastic bottles on a table and ask a child to push them off one by one as the song progresses. You could do the same with soft toys (*Ten fat teddies/sitting on a wall*) or children 'falling' off a wall of chairs (*Ten kind children ...*).

● ✿ Children count back from any given number between 20 to 0.

● ✿ Display a group of objects. *How many (objects, name) would there be if there was one fewer?* Repeat for different numbers and extend to 'two fewer'.

● ✿ Using either number cards/number picture cards and/or number name cards. *Which number is one fewer than 5?* Repeat for different numbers and extend to 'two fewer'.

● ✿ Count five cubes into a feely bag, then take three out. *How many are left?* Repeat using different amounts of cubes.

Introducing symbols
● Use '–' and '=' symbol cards and 1–6 number cards. A child chooses a number card (such as 4). *Which number is one fewer than four?* Introduce the '–' symbol by placing the '–' card beside the 4 number card and then the 1 number card: 4 – 1 *What is one fewer than four?* Now introduce the equals sign =: 4 – 1 = and, when the child has given the answer, place the 3: 4 – 1 = 3. Repeat for different numbers and extend to 'two fewer' for example 4 – 2 = 2.

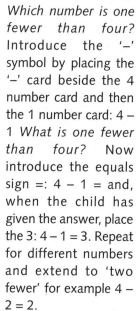

● Provide two sets of number cards (set one 5–9 and set two 1–4) and a '–' and '=' symbol cards. Ask the children to work in pairs. The first child chooses a card from set one (for example 6), then puts down the '–' card, the second child chooses a card from set two (for example 3) and puts down the '=' sign. Together both children work out the answer

Dice subtraction
● Using two dice, two children take turns to throw the dice, subtracting the smaller number from the larger number and choosing the corresponding number card.

● Use a dice or a spinner marked 1, 2, 3. Each child begins with 10 counters. In turn, children roll the dice or spin the spinner and take away the number shown from their pile. The winner is the person with the least number of counters after three turns.

● ☺ Children make up some subtraction number sentences (using symbols, pictures or apparatus) for 5.

● Use interlocking cubes for subtraction facts for 3, 4 and 5.

Follow a similar process to the addition facts – see page 52.

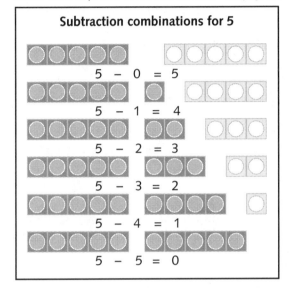

Subtraction combinations for 5

Solving number problems

Children should have experiences of addition and subtraction in a variety of contexts, including:
▶ money;
▶ length;
▶ mass;
▶ volume and capacity;
▶ time.

Data handling
Introducing criteria
● ☺ Working with the children, sort objects using different criteria but not more than one attribute, including:
▶ shape (*Let's pick out all the triangles.*);
▶ colour;
▶ size;
▶ will roll/will not roll;
▶ will bounce/will not bounce;
▶ can see through/ cannot see through;
▶ hard/soft;
▶ long/short.

● ☺ Working with the children, sort the class or group using different criteria in turn, including:
▶ sex;
▶ hair colour;
▶ length of hair;
▶ eye colour;
▶ coloured clothes;
▶ types of shoes;
▶ birthdays;
▶ members in the family;
▶ favourite pet;
▶ transportation to school.

● ☺ Sort objects/children without explaining your criteria. *How have I sorted these objects/children?*

● ☺ Children sort a group of objects using criteria chosen by you.

● ☺ Children sort a group of objects using their own criteria and say what their chosen criteria was.

Recording
● ☺ Children begin to record their sorting using a simple Venn diagram:

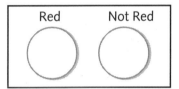

| Red | Not Red |

● ☺ Children begin to record their sorting using a simple Carroll diagram:

Blue	Not Blue

Shape, space and measures

Patterns and properties

Patterns
● Clap a rhythm pattern for children to copy. Ask individual children to clap a pattern for the rest of the class to copy.
Variation: Use percussion instruments.

● Make body patterns around the class, for example sitting, standing, hands on head, sitting, standing, hands on head.

● ☼ Ask children to sit in a circle. Give the first five children a coloured cube each to make a pattern (for example red, blue, red, blue, red). Ask the children to predict what colour cube the next child should be given. Continue around the circle. Repeat the activity using a different pattern, for example red, red, blue, red, red, blue, and so on. Repeat using 3/4/5 colours and using other apparatus and different criteria (size, shape).

● Children could sort out pieces of wallpaper or wrapping paper with repeating patterns. *How did you sort them?*

● ☼ Individual children can copy and continue patterns using different attributes (size, colour, shape).

● ☼ Encourage children to make and explain their own patterns involving objects, pictures, shapes and so on.

3D solids

● Children observe and collect items while on a walk around the classroom or school and discuss the objects they see along the way. They can then make a class book, wall display or mobile of their collections and observations.

● Children make models of a variety of objects, using Plasticine, play dough, clay or sand.

● Children sort wood offcuts according to thickness, mass, colour and so on. After completing and discussing their sorting, they could glue pieces together to make a model.

Naming, sorting and matching
● Examine a collection of 3D solids with the children, naming the shapes as you do so. Together, sort the shapes and display them with a name label for each group.

● Show the children a cube, name and label it and discuss its properties in relation to faces and corners.

● ☼ Children sort a collection of real 3D objects using shape criteria (boxes, tins and tubes).

● ☼ Children match real 3D objects of similar shape (a cereal box and a tea-bag box).

● ☼ Children sort 3D solids using shape criteria (cubes, cuboids, spheres and cylinders).

● ☼ Children match similar 3D solids (cubes, cuboids, spheres and cylinders).

● ☼ *Sort out these 3D solids. How did you do it?*

Identifying 3-D shapes
● ☼ Place a variety of 3D solids in a feely bag. Ask individual children to choose a shape and describe it while it is still in the bag. The rest of the class has to try and identify the shape, using other 3D models displayed in the room to help if necessary. When the class has identified the shape, the child pulls it out to see if they were correct.

● ☼ Children identify 3D solids in pictures, photographs, drawings and in the environment.

● ☼ *What am I?* Children describe three attributes of any object, using their new shape vocabulary where possible, and the other children have to try and identify the object.

● Children build a 3D model of a cube.

2D shapes
Children use all the faces of various objects such as fruit, vegetables, stones or boxes to make prints.

Naming, sorting and matching
● Examine a collection of 2D shapes with the children, naming the shapes as you do so. Together, sort the shapes and display them with a label on each group.

● Children can:
▶ make a shape book using cut-outs from newspapers and magazines, go on a shape hunt and place cut-outs of various shapes (squares, rectangles, circles, triangles) onto real objects;
▶ trace around the faces of various objects;
▶ make shape pictures using various media (pencils, crayons, paints, fabric).

Squares
● Show a square to the children, name it and label it. Discuss its properties.

● Show a shape that is not a square to them and ask: *Why is this shape not a square?* Discuss why it is not a square.

● Make Venn and Carroll diagrams involving shapes that are squares and are not squares.

Rectangles, circles, triangles
● Repeat the above activity, showing and naming rectangles, circles and triangles.

● Make a Venn and Carroll diagram involving shapes that are rectangles and circles, triangles and squares, circles and triangles, and so on.

● ✪ Ask children to identify squares, rectangles, triangles and circles in pictures, drawings and in the environment.

● ✪ *Sort out these 2D shapes. How did you do it?*

Matching 2D shape game
● Two children shuffle a variety of 2D shape cards together (2x squares, rectangles, circles, triangles) and play Pelmanism with them. *Variations:* Use irregular as well as regular squares, rectangles, circles (ovals), triangles.

Position and movement
Position
● Use soft toys and a box with a lid. Help the children to find the right words to describe the positions in which you put the toys and the box, for example: *near, close, far, to the left, to the right, in front of, behind, beside, next, next to, above, across, along, around, after, back to back, before, behind, beside, top, bottom, centre, close, down, up, far, forward, further, from, here, high, low, in, inside, into, first, last, middle, near, on, onto, on top of, outside, over, past, right over, round, side by side, there, through, top, turn, under, over, underneath, up, upside down.*

Children can then take turns to position the toys in response to suggestions from you or the rest of the class.

● ✪ Ask children to use the position vocabulary to describe position in models, pictures, photographs and sketches. *Where is the man standing?*

● Children draw the position of objects in a model/a simple plan of the classroom.

Left and right
Most children find it difficult to distinguish left from right.

● Have a 'left' day or a 'right' day, where various things are done using only the left or right hand (putting up your hand, fetching a book).

● Ask them to look at the backs of their hands with their fingers together and thumbs spread out. *Which hand makes a capital 'L' for left ?*

● Sing the song 'One, two, three, four, five, Once I caught a fish alive', and check to make sure that everyone holds up 'This little finger on the right'. (Don't forget to face the same way as the children because, if you are facing the class, your right hand will be on their left!)

Movement
● Take the class into the playground or hall. Tell them that they are robots that cannot move without being given directions. Give them the directions yourself to begin with (*The robots move two steps forward* and so on) and then let the children take turns to do it.

● ✪ Children draw a simple plan of the route from the classroom to the hall/playground.

● Children use ICT equipment such as a Turtle or Roamer to show movement.

Measures

Length

Children:

‣ cut a length of string into short/long pieces;

‣ tie pieces of string together to make one length;

‣ unroll/untangle a piece of string or rope. *(Does the length change when it is unrolled?)*;

‣ draw a long/short/straight/curved line and discuss its length;

‣ go on a length hunt in the classroom/school and find objects that are long/short;

‣ make long and short objects using Plasticine;

‣ make a book about long and short objects using drawings and pictures from newspapers and magazines.

Comparisons

● ✪ Hold up various pairs of objects (pencils, ribbons, paintbrushes). *Which is the longer? Which is the shorter?*

● ✪ Ask children to use their bodies to measure things, finding objects which are longer than their foot, shorter than their little finger and so on.

● ✪ Compare the distance between various objects in the classroom. Find out the distance between the door and the bookcase, or the door and the teacher's desk. *Which is the longer? Which is the shorter? How can we check to see if we are right?*

● ✪ Compare the height of various children. *Who is shorter? Who is taller?* Repeat using various objects such as towers of cubes, sticks or boxes.

Non-standard units

● ✪ Measure the:

‣ length of a desk using pencils;

‣ distance between the desk and the door using paces;

‣ height of a child using crayons.

● ✪ Children measure the length, distance and height of various objects in the classroom using Unifix cubes, pencils or other items in the classroom.

● Have an estimation table in the classroom. *How long is that piece of ribbon? How did you make your estimate?*

● Using newspaper and sticky tape, see which group/pair of children can make the tallest tower.

Conservation of length

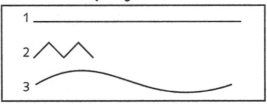

● ✪ For each set of lines ask: *Which piece of string is longer?*

● ✪ Children order various objects according to their length and height.

Mass

● ✪ Ask children to feel objects of different mass, such as a feather and a bag of flour. *Which is heavier? Which is lighter?*

● Children find objects which are light and heavy.

● ✪ Ask children to find something heavier/lighter than a book. *Show me how you know it's heavier/lighter?*

● ✪ Children order objects of various sizes according to their mass.

Conservation of mass

● ✪ Children have two pieces of Plasticine that are of the same mass rolled into balls of a similar size. Ask them to make a sausage with each piece of Plasticine. *Is the mass the same in each sausage?*

● ✪ Have a collection of objects of various masses. Use objects that are: small and heavy, small and light, large and heavy, large and light. Ask children to describe the mass of the objects in relation to each other and to their size.

● Set up an estimation table. *How heavy is that tin? Will it be lighter or heavier than the block?* Ask the children to explain how they made their estimate.

Volume and capacity

● ✪ Show children three containers of the same size. Fill one full of water, another half full and leave the third empty. Ask the children to describe the amount of water in each container. Repeat using sand, cubes or marbles.

● ✪ Pour water from a jug into a small cup until it overflows. *Which holds more water – the jug or the cup?*

● Children order containers of various sizes according to their capacity.

● Have an estimation table in the classroom. *How much water would this container hold? How did you make your estimate?*

Conservation of capacity

● Give the children two containers which have the same capacity but which are different shapes. *Will these containers hold the same amount?* The children pour the liquid from one container to the other to check their answer.

Time

Discuss with the children the concept of time using the following vocabulary: *daytime, night-time, yesterday, today, tomorrow, all day, a long while, a little while, morning, afternoon, evening, night, now, later, before, after.*

Daily routine

● Talk about the daily routine: in the morning before school, at school, when they leave school in the afternoon.

● Children make a chart of things that they do during the day and at night, in the morning and in the afternoon.

Ordering

● Children order events in a story or nursery rhyme such as 'Humpty Dumpty' or 'Jack and the Beanstalk'.

● ✪ Discuss and order the events of the day.

● ✪ Discuss and order events over a week.

Length of time

Children engage in different activities and the length of time for the activities are compared. Present the findings like this:

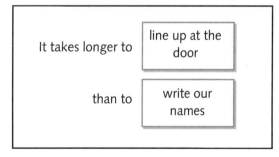

● Ask the children to think of things that they can do in a long time/short time.

● Supply a collection of books of about the same size. *Who can make a pile of 20 books most quickly? How did you decide?*

Mathematics

Days of the week

● Introduce the names of the days of the week. Make a chart identifying specific things that happen at school on certain days of the week. Illustrate it to help to remind children of events each day.

● Make a chart to display the days of the week and reinforce the concept of 'yesterday', 'today' and 'tomorrow'. Use sticky-back Velcro on the backs of the 'day' cards and on the spaces in the chart. Each day a different child updates the chart:

Yesterday was	Tuesday
Today is	Wednesday
Tomorrow will be	Thursday

● ✪ Children order a set of cards with the days of the week written on them.

Measuring time

● Measure time using various non-standard measures. How many times can you:
▶ build a tower of ten bricks;
▶ walk to the cloakroom and back;
▶ take off a shoe and put it on while the sand timer/water timer runs?

● Using a one-minute sand timer:
▶ how high a tower can you make using cubes;
▶ how many books can you stack into a pile?

Clock time

● Show the children an analogue clock. Talk about clocks. Count the numbers. Talk about the 'hands' on a clock.

● Introduce 'o'clock' using the analogue clock. Talk about important times of the day that feature 'o'clock'. (*We start school at 9 o'clock in the morning.*)

● ✪ The children draw pictures that correspond with important times of the day that feature o'clock, then they fill in hands on a clock face stamped beside their pictures and write the time in words.

🎈 Assessment

Children demonstrate the outcomes of their learning through speaking, writing, drawing and engaging in other activities.

You need a variety of assessment strategies to help you to establish where your children are in their learning and what they need to do next. Whatever assessment strategies you use, it is important to ensure that tasks are appropriate to the individual child and that they are directly related to the learning objectives.

The levels of expectation suggested at the beginning of this chapter (see page 43) provide a comprehensive checklist for assessing your children's learning at the end of the reception year and the activities that have the ✪ next to them in the Practical ideas section are suitable assessment activities.

Science

Teaching science to the under-fives may seem a very formal requirement, but young children have enquiring minds and are curious about everything around them. It comes naturally for young children to try things out, to see how things work, manipulate, feel, be curious, to ask questions and seek answers and these are exactly the attributes of a good scientist.

Reception children can be involved in any science activity with an appropriate interest value which has the capacity to excite, satisfy their natural curiosity and provide enjoyment. The emphasis in these early science activities should be to provide a first-hand investigative learning approach, with the children's interests and experience kept very firmly in mind. Guidance on teaching science to reception children comes from the Knowledge and understanding of the world section of the *Early learning goals* document (QCA) as well as from the early stages of the National Curriculum.

Early learning goals

The Early learning goals document sets out goals for learning for children by the end of the foundation stage (the end of the reception year). The area of learning entitled 'Knowledge and understanding of the world' is a precursor to Key Stage 1 science, design and technology, ICT, history and geography. The early learning goals for children at the end of the foundation stage in the area of science (within the area of learning, 'Knowledge and understanding of the world') include: '... *using all the senses as appropriate to investigate objects and materials; finding out about and identifying features of living things, objects and events; looking closely at patterns, change, similarities and differences and asking questions about why things work and how things happen.*'

The National Curriculum

The reception class also provides an opportunity to prepare children for the National Curriculum.

Although the National Curriculum specifies what areas of science must be taught at Key Stage 1, each school can decide in which order the Programmes of Study are introduced. To

Look closely at similarities and differences

meet the statutory requirements all units must be covered at some stage during Key Stage 1, and children will then have covered the appropriate work and be able to undertake the assessment at the end of that Key Stage.

What should they be able to do?

The requirements for Science in the National Curriculum are set down in four sections. When we examine these, it is easy to be lulled into believing that the three sections dealing with knowledge and understanding put the emphasis on the content of science rather than the process.

This notion is soon dispelled by the realisation that *Scientific Enquiry (Sc1)* is regarded as having roughly equal importance to the other three science sections combined. Although it offers no facts to be learned, Sc1 will only be achieved over a period of time, perhaps the whole of the primary school stage, or even longer. The aim is for children to develop an understanding of scientific phenomena through systematic and practical exploration and investigation.

Scientific enquiry

Scientific enquiry within the National Curriculum at Key Stage 1 is broken down into several components that cover 'ideas and evidence', and 'investigative skills' that include planning, and obtaining and presenting evidence.

Planning

Planning includes asking questions and predicting. It is important to provide plenty of opportunities that promote discussion between the children themselves and between the children and the teacher. The children should be encouraged to ask questions of the *Who? What? Where? When? Why? How many? How much? How far?* variety.

Children will not automatically come up with ideas that can be investigated without prior practice and without having begun to develop an idea of what constitutes a scientific investigation.

In the reception class, the children's predictions will often simply be a guess, which is not based upon any scientific knowledge or scientific analysis. Only later, after practice in carrying out appropriate investigations, activities and discussion, will children acquire a basic scientific knowledge and learn to make predictions that are based on this knowledge and previous experience and the data they have collected.

Obtaining evidence

Children should be encouraged to use all their senses to measure and record accurately. Most reception children will be limited to describing the simple features of objects, living things and the events they observe.

Considering and presenting evidence

This includes interpreting the results of any investigation and evaluating the scientific evidence. Encourage your children to make comparisons, to look for patterns and to communicate their findings in a variety of ways. This gives them a great opportunity to share their thinking and to relate their understanding to scientific knowledge.

At this stage, most children's consideration of evidence will be limited to communicating findings in simple ways through talking, and making drawings or simple charts. They should also be given opportunities to use ICT. Remember that over-emphasis on recording, particularly the use of writing, can stifle children's investigative tendencies at this young age.

Knowledge and understanding

The three sections of the Programme of Study dealing with knowledge and understanding are *Sc2: Life Processes and Living Things*; *Sc3: Materials and their Properties*; and *Sc4: Physical Processes*. These are instantly recognisable as the biology, chemistry and physics of secondary school days. (Remember that the Programmes of Study are not always intended to show progression, and the letters a, b, c, and so on, do not always imply increasing complexity.)

Breadth of study

There is a fifth area of National Curriculum science which has no distinct title. It comes as an Introduction to each Key Stage description and sets down guidelines that can be applied to all science work. This fifth area applies across scientific enquiry, Life Processes and Living Things, Materials and their Properties, and Physical Processes. It highlights many important cross-curricular aspects of science.

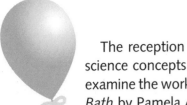

Science

The reception class provides an opportunity to introduce children to a broad range of science concepts and activities although there are few opportunities at this early stage to examine the work of great scientists in much detail. However, stories such as *Mr Archimedes' Bath* by Pamela Allen (Puffin) provide good starting points.

The so-called 'Fifth area' of science at Key Stage 1 - 'Breadth of study', covers the following:
● relating science to a range of familiar domestic and environmental contexts, as well as looking at how science has led to the development of many useful things;
● referring to a range of sources of information and data (including ICT-based sources) and using the information to carry out investigations;
● communicating ideas using simple scientific language and recording techniques;
● recognising and controlling risks in science work (health and safety).

Science content at KS1

Within the National Curriculum at Key Stage 1, the three knowledge and understanding sections of the Programmes of Study are sub-divided as follows:

Sc2: Life processes and living things

● Life processes
● Humans and other animals
● Green plants
● Variation and classification
● Living things in their environment

Sc3: Materials and their properties

● Grouping materials
● Changing materials

Sc4: Physical processes

● Electricity
● Forces and motion
● Light and sound

Teaching ideas

The activities which follow under Practical ideas have been divided up into these three main areas of knowledge and understanding. This division is very loose since, for example, moulding clay to change its shape could be considered as work on a material (Sc3) or using a force to change the shape of something (Sc4). As mentioned previously, there is no set order for teaching the various topics and the children's spontaneous interests, or even the prevailing weather conditions (in the case of outdoor work on living things), may well help you to decide when to start a particular topic.

All the activities suggested here are well tried and tested, but practical science, like all practical subjects, does have the potential to be dangerous. Teachers should consult the Association for Science Education booklet *Be Safe* and check that they have fulfilled local safety requirements before attempting any activity which causes them concern.

Practical ideas

 ## Making a start

There are many ways of introducing Science topics to children in a reception class. Some starting points are suggested here and there are further ideas in the Ideas bank on page 71.

All about me

Let each child start a book or chart called 'All about me'. Help them to fill in information about their name, address, age, measurements, any other personal information they can think of, using pictures to illustrate their contributions.

Include further information such as 'What I can do best', 'My favourite game/story/toy/TV programme', portraits of the children and their family and friends, their first words as a baby and any other information they would like to add.

Walks

● Take a walk around the school, or make a visit to a farm or park together, and discuss with the children the various living things they have seen. Help them to decide whether each living thing is a plant or an animal.

● Go on a listening walk around the school or neighbourhood. *What sounds can you hear? Can you tell where the sounds are coming from? Are the sounds loud or soft?*

Collections

● Collect pictures of as many plants and animals (including humans) as possible. Stick them on card and let the children group them into sets on the basis of things such as plants/animals, shape, colour, number of legs and so on.

● Make a collection of objects, or pictures of objects, which give out light, such as torches, candles, light bulbs, lanterns and the sun. Discuss with the children what these objects are and which of them they could play with. Warn them of the dangers of looking directly at the sun.

Properties of sand

Encourage the children to make full use of the sand tray to make discoveries about the properties of sand. Provide a range of tools and equipment for them to use. Ask them why they think damp sand is better for creating shapes. *What do you think sand is made of? How are wet and dry sand different? Which is heavier, a carton of wet sand or a carton of dry sand? Why? Try pouring and sieving wet and dry sand.* Let them try making prints in wet and dry sand with different objects.

Push and pull

Look at a variety of toys that move, and discuss with the children how they move. Sort them into toys that are pulled and toys that are pushed. They could also be sorted into toys that are moved by pushes or pulls from within (by motors and springs), and toys which are moved by outside pushes or pulls.

 ## Developing key areas

Life processes and living things

Humans as organisms

● Show the children a cardboard cut-out, a shop dummy or some other model of the human body. Let the children take it in turns to point to the main external features of the body, naming the parts that they know (ankle, arm, body, elbow, fingers, foot, hand, knee, leg, toes, neck,

shoulder, cheek, chin, ear, eye, forehead, hair, mouth, nose). *Can you name the main parts of the body of a doll or teddy bear?*

● Help the children to learn the names of the parts of their bodies by singing the songs 'Heads, Shoulders, Knees and Toes'.

● The most effective and straightforward approach to human variation is to ask the question: *How big are we?* Let the children measure each others' height and weight and make simple bar charts to show the results. Exercise sensitivity to the children at all times when making comparisons or comments about their bodies.

Try other measurements such as how high each child can reach while standing on tip-toe. Let the children draw around the outstretched fingers of one hand and carefully cut out the resulting shape. Compare the sizes of hands by laying the shapes on top of each other. *Who has the largest hand? Whose hand is smallest?* At the end of this activity draw attention to the fact that no two children are exactly the same. Emphasise the value of each child.

● Discuss with the children the features everyone has in common (two eyes, two ears, nose, mouth) but how everyone's face looks different. Get them to work in pairs with a plastic mirror and compare their features in turn.

● Ask a child to describe a friend's face without revealing who is being described. Suggest that hair colour and style, eye colour and shape of the face can be described. Ask the other children to guess who it is.

● Ask the children to bring in photographs of themselves as babies. Make a display (don't forget to include your own baby photo). *Can you guess who's who?*

● Make a collection of clothes, toys and shoes (or pictures of these objects). Divide the items into three groups, according to whether the garments are for people younger, older or the same age as the children. Discuss how they have changed since they were babies wearing bibs and nappies. *What other changes will have happened by the time you wear adult's shoes?*

● Discuss why we eat food. *Why do we feel hungry?* Make a survey of the children's favourite foods under the headings *meat, fruit, fish, bread, puddings* and use a tally. Record the results visually, with either a bar chart, a mapping chart or a set chart. Encourage the children to find other ways to record their results.

● Discuss how the food we eat is changed by cooking. *What other things are done to our food when it is prepared?* Refer to washing, cutting, slicing, peeling, grating, freezing, melting and thawing.

● Talk about the different ways we can move: hopping, skipping, jumping, on knees, on toes, on bottoms, backwards, forwards and sideways. Talk about the different parts of the body used in movement. You could follow this up with practical work in PE.

● Talk about what happens to your body when you feel cold (teeth chatter, you shiver, your hands feel numb). *Which parts of your body get cold first? What do you do to warm yourself up?* (Put on extra clothes, put on heating in the room, take hot foods or drinks, take exercise, rub hands together, have a hot bath.)

Plants

Safety: Be careful to ask parents about any known allergies before letting children handle plants or parts of plants. Ensure they wash their hands thoroughly afterwards.

● Build up a large and varied collection of plants in your classroom. Let the children closely observe the plants and make them responsible for watering them. Encourage them to examine each plant and identify the leaves, flowers, stems and, where appropriate, roots.

● Ask some volunteers to bring a flower to school. *Are the flowers as fresh and the stems as rigid once they are in class as they were when the flowers were first picked?* Stand the flowers in water and watch them return to a more upright stance. (You may need to give badly-wilted flowers the support of a cylinder of newspaper to help them return to an upright position.) *What has made the flowers stand up? How do you know?*

● Show the children how water is actually taken up into the stems of flowers. Add a few drops of ink or food colouring to water in a container, cut the stems of a few white or pale-coloured flowers and stand them in the dyed water. Leave them for a day or so and watch how the flowers become coloured with the dye.

● Stand a stick of celery in a container of dyed water, and show the children the tiny 'tubes' that carry water up the plant. Cut across the stem every day or so to show the children how far the coloured water has travelled up the stem.

● Make a collection of fruit stones, pips and seeds. After warning the children about the dangers of putting these in their mouths, ears or up their noses let them examine the different varieties. Can they find ways of grouping the seeds – large/small, fat/thin, wrinkly/smooth, roll/do not roll? Make collage pictures by sticking seeds on outline drawings made on pieces of card.

● The pips of oranges, lemons, tangerines and grapefruit will germinate quite quickly and produce attractive plants. Plant several in a shallow pot or tub filled with moist compost. The children can then transplant them into individual pots when the first true leaves appear. Shelled (unsalted) peanuts will also germinate, but need to be kept in a warm place.

● Grow pea, runner bean or broad bean seeds in pots of moist compost or soil kept on a sunny window-sill. Loosely fill clear glass or plastic containers with moist soil or compost, and then gently push the seeds down between the soil or compost and the walls of the container. Cover the outside of the container with black paper or plastic which can be removed for a short time each day so that the children can observe how the seedlings are growing. Loosely tie the seedlings to thin sticks when they grow tall. Measure the growth of the seedlings each week. Tell the story of 'Jack and the Beanstalk'.

● Seeds can be grown in all sorts of containers: polystyrene and metal foil food trays, yoghurt pots, egg boxes, margarine tubs, ice-cream containers and the bases of plastic squash bottles to name a few. Seeds will germinate on moist cotton wool, paper, tissues, paper towels, flannel or cloth, as well as in moist soil or seed compost. They will need to be transferred to soil or compost if you wish to grow the plants on. Assist good propagation by putting the seed container inside a plastic bag which helps to conserve the moisture and maintain an even temperature.

● Show the full life history of a plant by growing one from a seed to adult plant and then back to seed again. (Radishes and wild groundsel plants have short life cycles.)

● Press leaves and make a mounted collection. Lay colourful, undamaged leaves neatly between sheets of newspaper and press them down with books or heavy weights for several days. Remove the leaves when they are dry and brittle, and mount and label them on large sheets of card or paper.

● Collect large leaves and lay them, vein sides upwards, on a table. Let the children make rubbings of them using a wax crayon or soft pencil. The leaves can also be used as a mask, by laying them on a sheet of paper and spraying or splattering paint around them. Carefully remove the leaves to reveal a white leaf shape.

● If there is a tree in the school grounds the children can draw it and label the parts – trunk, branches, twigs, leaves, flowers and roots (if visible). Take rubbings from the bark.

● Some plants can be propagated from cuttings. Sprigs of busy Lizzy (Impatiens), tradescantia, and garden mint will quickly send out roots if put in a bottle full of water on a sunny window-sill. Bulbs, such as onions, hyacinths or daffodils will also flourish if placed in a hyacinth glass of water or in a jar of water; keep the water level just below the base of the bulb.

● Place a selection of vegetable 'tops' in saucers of water. Try carrot, turnip and swede. Observe root growth and talk about how plants take in water through their roots.

Livings things in the environment

● Search all the 'cosy corners' around the school grounds, looking in crevices, under stones and wood, in tussocks of grass, under heaps of dead tree leaves and other places for minibeasts. Carefully collect one of each kind you find. Do not handle the minibeasts but use a plastic spoon and small brush to transfer them into collecting pots. Let the children examine the minibeasts with hand lenses or magnifying glasses. *What colour is each minibeast? How many legs does it have? What kind of minibeast is it? How many ways of grouping the creatures can you think of?* Return the minibeasts to the places where they were found after they have been studied in this way.

● If your school only has an asphalt playground, you may still be able to find animals in cracks and crevices and in moss, but try also to visit a local park (check your planned activity with the park-keeper first) or, better still, arrange a trip to a country centre.

Materials and their properties

● Display pieces of common materials, both natural and manufactured. Let the children observe and describe the materials and then find as many ways as possible of grouping them into sets; including by shape, colour and texture.

● Make a 'feely box' containing different kinds of materials (that are safe for the children to handle). Ask the children to describe what each material feels like. *How many of the items can you identify by touch alone?*

● Discuss with the children the many uses of water (drinking, cooking, washing, swimming, playing, plant growth). *Where does water come from?* (Briefly explain the so-called water cycle.) Put a plastic jar in the playground and measure the amount of rain which falls every day. *Where does the rain water go to?* Draw around a puddle in the playground with chalk. Observe what happens to it after a few hours. Keep observing the shape of the puddle at regular intervals.

● Put equal amounts of water in an open jar, an identical closed jar and on a saucer and leave them on a window-sill. See what happens to the water after a few hours, overnight and over a couple of days. Record, with pictures, the time taken for the water to evaporate from the open containers.

● Look at different water levels in different sized containers. Measure water up to the same point in two identical plastic bottles, then transfer the water into different sized and shaped transparent containers. *Which has the most water in?* Many young children will not be able to grasp this concept (conservation of volume) right away and will need to experiment repeatedly.

● Soak equal-sized strips of various fabrics in water and put them to dry on the window-sill. Feel the fabrics at regular intervals and discuss which fabrics dry quickest and slowest. Record in pictures and note the time it takes for each fabric to dry. Talk about whether sunshine and shade, indoors or outdoors would make any difference to the speed of drying. Make fair tests by placing equal amounts of water on equal-sized pieces of the same material. Place one inside, one in the sun, one in the wind and one in the shade. *Which one dries first? Why? Where does the water go to?*

● Discuss what happens when a sugar lump is placed in water. Place a lump in a cup of water, wait a while, then stir the water. *Where does the sugar go to? Will the sugar dissolve (or disappear) faster in warm water than in cold water?* Try it and see.

● Let the children look at and touch a selection of pebbles. Talk about their size, shape, texture, pattern and colour. Sort the pebbles and make pictures with them by embedding them in sand, clay or Plasticine. Use pebbles for balancing and weighing activities.

● Introduce the concept of solids and liquids. Discuss with the children which foods and drinks are solids and which are liquids. Ask questions such as, *Does this food 'flow'? Can this food sit on the table or on a piece of paper? Could someone without teeth eat this food? Could we keep this food in a bottle?*

● Look closely at ice-cubes. *How do they look, feel and taste? Where in the classroom will they melt the quickest? Where will the ice-cubes last longest?*

● Discuss the differences between hot and cold. Let the children describe how they feel in hot weather and in cold weather. *What do you do to keep cool in hot weather? What do you do to keep warm in cold weather?* Look at the clothes people wear in very hot and very cold countries and see what distinguishes them (thickness, type of fabric, colours, style). Link the discussion with hot and cold food (relating the foods to the weather). *How can you tell whether food is hot or cold?* (Steaming, bubbling in the pan, frosty from the freezer, hard, soft.)

● Examine slices of white bread together and write down the words the children use to describe the bread. Then toast slices of bread for different lengths of time. *How is the bread different? What does toasting do to bread? Can we turn the bread back to how it was originally?* (If the children are to be allowed to taste the bread and toast, you must, of course, ensure that strict hygienic conditions are maintained.)

● Investigate pliable materials, such as play dough, Plasticine, clay, Blu-tack, dough. Give the children time to enjoy the different textures and their pliability. Ask the children to make a figure or some other recognisable shape with each type of material. *Which is the best material for making models? Are some of the materials too hard or too soft?*

● Provide the children with a variety of mixtures, such as sand and pebbles, rice and sugar, rice and water, flour and raisins, beads of different sizes. Let them experiment to find different ways of sorting or separating the components of these mixtures. They should record their results in pictorial form. Encourage them to devise their own sorting equipment, for example a cardboard box with holes of different sizes made in the bottom, or a paper chute with holes cut in it to sort beads of different sizes.

Physical processes
Electricity

● Make a collection of pictures of electrical devices cut out from magazines and catalogues. Sort them into sets using a variety of criteria such as: motor/non-motor; light/heat/movement; mains/battery, and so on.

● Collect together some battery-powered devices such as toys, torches and radios. With your help, the children can examine the devices to see where the batteries are. Discuss why we sometimes use electricity from batteries and sometimes from the mains. Make use of this opportunity to reinforce the safety message that, while it is perfectly safe to experiment with torch batteries, they should **never** experiment with mains electricity.

● For a large wall display, draw the outline of a house and then include cut-out pictures or the children's drawings of various items of domestic electrical equipment in the correct rooms.

Forces and motion
Sinking and floating

● Introduce the topic with a practical question which the children will relate to. *Who can swim and/or float, with or without armbands? How do the armbands stop you from sinking?*

● Collect different objects from around the classroom and put them, one by one, in the water tray to see if they will float or sink. Ask the children to guess if each item will float or sink, before it is put in the water, and to give reasons why. *Which things floated and which sank?* Put all items that floated into one set, and all the ones that sank into another set. Compare the objects in the two sets and discuss what the items are made of. Then discuss what makes them float or sink. *Do all big things sink? Do all small things float? Do all wooden things float? Do all plastic things float? Do all metal things sink?*

● Use clay, Plasticine or metal foil to make a variety of shapes. Put these shapes on water and observe which shapes and materials float and which sink. The children can record their findings in pictures. Discuss which shapes floated best and which materials made the best floater.

● Make a collection of pieces of different kinds of wood. Ask the children to investigate whether all wood floats. *Do all kinds of wood float equally well?*

Pushing and pulling
● Visit a local park or children's playground as a stimulus to talk about going to the playground. If this is not practical, find some catalogue pictures of play equipment to discuss with the children. Look closely at the slide. Discuss walking up the steps and sliding down. *Which is easier? Which is quicker?* Now examine the swings, roundabouts and other rides and games. *Which do we move by pushing? Which do we move by pulling? Which can we move by a push or a pull?*

● Investigate the different ways of moving a large box along the floor. Try pulling, pushing, using rollers or wheels, or any other ideas the children have.

● Let the children examine a collection of toy cars. Can they find out what makes them move?

● Investigate toy cars. *Which one travels furthest on a flat, level surface? Do you always obtain the same result? Is your test fair? If you add a weight, such as a piece of Plasticine, to the car does it make a difference? Does the surface on which the car is rolled make a difference?*

● Using a collection of wheeled toys, ask the children to predict which will travel furthest with one push. Ask them to suggest ways of testing them fairly. Try out their suggestions. *Which toy travels furthest?*

● Use Duplo, LEGO, Bauplay or other modelling kits to make wheeled vehicles. Test them on different slopes and different surfaces.

● What is the best shape for a wheel? Let the children make different shaped wheels from cardboard. Observe how the different shapes move.

Light
● Go on a 'light-spotting' walk. Look for different kinds of lights, such as the sun (remind the children not to look directly at the sun as it could damage their eyes), street lights, car headlights, hazard warning lights, electric neon signs and any others you can locate. *In what ways are they the same, and in what ways are they different?*

● Discuss the differences between being in a room when it is light and when it is dark.

● Blindfold one volunteer child and ask another to lead him or her around the classroom. Discuss the problems of not being able to see because everything is dark. *What would it be like to be blind?*

● Use a torch to sort objects according to whether they are shiny or dull. *Can you make a dull object shiny? Can you make a shiny object dull?*

● Talk about what shadows are and when we can see them. *How do you make your shadow change its shape? How can you lose your shadow? Can you make a tall, short, wide or narrow shadow? Can you make a funny or frightening shadow?*

● Can the children make shadows indoors? Using an overhead projector or slide projector in a darkened room, show them how to make hand shapes on the wall. Let them investigate how the size of a shadow can be changed (by varying the distance of the object from the light source). Using a slide projector, cast the shadows of children's faces (in profile) on the wall. They will have to keep still! Trace these silhouettes onto black sugar paper with a white crayon, and cut them out.

● Let pairs of children take it in turns to play in the dark under a cloth-covered table. Provide them with a torch, plastic mirrors and coloured Cellophane. After each pair has experimented for a set period of time, let them tell the others what they found out.

Sound

● Let the children compare what sounds they can hear in the classroom with and without their ears covered.

● *What sounds can you make with your body?* (Stamping, clapping, whistling, talking and clicking fingers are just a few possibilities.) *Can you make a sound without moving any part of you?* Children who make sounds with their voice without moving their lips will have to be assured that, nonetheless, their vocal chords are vibrating. They probably won't believe you, but if they put their fingers on their throats they should be able to feel the vibrations.

● Collect toys that make a noise such as rattles, squeaking toys, computer games and musical instruments. *Are the sounds high or low, loud or soft, long or short?* Ask the children to think of words to describe the different sounds.

● Let the children design and make their own musical instruments from old containers, such as yoghurt pots and plastic bottles. *Who can devise the most unusual instrument?*

● The children can make music by using materials and objects which can be found around the classroom, including pencil cases, tidy boxes, pencils, cardboard containers, rulers, cups and bottles.

● Make a collection of eight sealed yoghurt pots with two of each containing stones, beads, nails and sand. Can the children match the pairs just by shaking the contents?

● Ask the children to sit in silence and run a sand timer or kitchen timer for a minute. *How many sounds did you hear during that time?* Make a tape of sounds heard around the school (the playground at break, the bell, footsteps, teachers talking, a tap running) for the children to identify. Sort the sounds into long/short, high/low, loud/soft, whether the children like/dislike the sounds.

💡 Ideas bank

● Set up a bird table in the school grounds. Keep it well supplied with table scraps, seeds, nuts and other foods (not desiccated coconut or salted peanuts). Limit the quantity of food put out in the spring (when young birds are learning to forage) and don't put bread or nuts out in the spring as young birds can choke on these. Let the children take it in turns to keep a daily record of the number of birds of each species which visit the bird table. Plot simple bar charts of their findings.

● Study the life cycle of a dandelion plant, beginning with seeds collected from a dandelion 'clock'. Plant them in containers of moist soil or compost. The children can keep a 'dandelion diary' to show what happens.

● Compare how different-coloured clothes show up in poor light conditions. One way to demonstrate this is for the children to shine a torch on each item of clothing in turn under a covered table. Discuss the road safety implications of this investigation. Ask if any of the children wear special clothing when they are out at night.

● Make a collection of (old) gloves. Include rubber, cotton, fur, wool and leather. Test which kind of gloves keep our hands warmest. One way to do this is to hold ice-cubes in the gloved hand and to time how long it is before the cold is felt through the glove.

● Provide a wide variety of water toys including containers, pumps, funnels, tubing, sponges and syringes. *How many ways can you find of making water move?*

● Have a ping-pong ball race. *Who can make their ping-pong ball go the furthest by squirting water at it? What makes the best squirter?* (This activity is best carried out on the playground on a fine day!)

● *How far can you squeeze water from a squeezy bottle? How can you measure how far the water goes?* (Another activity for outdoors!)

● Make a display of different kinds of paper and to show different uses of paper. Can the children devise a way of comparing the strengths of different kinds of paper? Help them to ensure their tests are fair by providing them with equal-sized strips of the different kinds of paper to be compared.

● Make ice lollies by freezing fruit drinks or juices in different-shaped containers. Melt butter or chocolate in different-shaped containers, allow the molten substance to solidify and compare the resulting shapes and textures.

● Let the children experiment with clay – moulding, rolling, flattening and shaping it. They could try joining pieces of clay together by various methods, including wetting it. *How can you make the strongest join?* Discuss what the clay feels like. Let them compare baked clay with unbaked.

● Make a simple dough by mixing flour and water. Examine its shape, colour and texture. Bake some of the dough and compare the resulting unleavened bread with the unbaked dough. *Is it possible to turn the baked bread back into the dough?*

● Add different substances, one at a time, to water. Ask the children to predict and record what happens. (Try sand, glass marbles, sugar, salt, flour, rice, pebbles and poster paint powder.) *What happens if liquids such as milk, cooking oil or vinegar are added to water?*

● Let the children examine a torch. They could take it to pieces and draw the various parts. *What happens if the batteries are put back the wrong way? Does the torch still work?* Try putting discs of different materials, such as paper, plastic, foil or a coin, between the batteries. *Does the torch work now?*

● Find out how the shadows of familiar objects change when they are held in different ways in sunlight. (Choose objects with simple, easily recognisable shapes such as a broom, an umbrella, a teddy bear and a chair.)

● Let the children take it in turns to pull a volunteer who is wearing ordinary shoes and then roller skates. *What differences do you notice?*

● Provide a collection of balls. Ask the children to sort them by size, colour, weight, bounciness and any other criteria they can think of.

● Investigate whether the height from which a ball is dropped makes a difference as to how high and how many times it bounces.

● Let the children investigate the movement of small toy cars down a slope (a short plank with one end resting on books). Ask them to predict what will happen if the angle of the slope is changed. *How can you make your test fair?*

Assessment

At the end of each topic you will have a good idea whether the children enjoyed the work and which style of teaching was most effective. Overall you will be able to evaluate each topic against the criteria with which you started, so by the end of the year you should also be able to judge how much the children have learned.

What do they know?

There is no set list of facts which children should know by this stage, but all the children should have gained some scientific knowledge this year.

At the end of their time in the reception class you might expect the majority of children to know:

- that there are many different kinds of plants and animals (Sc2);
- the names of the main external parts of the body, expressed verbally (Sc2);
- the main parts of a plant (Sc2);
- how to sort the different groups of plants and animals, from their shape and appearance (Sc2);
- that there are lots of different materials (Sc3);
- the main differences between materials, such as rough/smooth, soft/hard, cold/hot, shiny/dull (Sc3);
- that many materials can change shape (Sc3);
- that cooking changes food (Sc3);
- that some everyday appliances use electricity (Sc4);
- how to sort electrical equipment into groups (Sc4);
- the dangers associated with electricity (Sc4);
- the difference between a push and a pull (Sc4);
- if things are moving fast or slow, and which way they will go when pushed or pulled (Sc4);

- that some objects float and some sink (Sc4);
- that some things give out light (Sc4);
- an opaque object is necessary for a shadow to be formed (Sc4);
- that there are many kinds of sounds and sources of sounds (Sc4);
- that some sounds are loud and some are soft (Sc4).

What can they do?

Children should be able to:
- describe objects and materials (Sc1);
- describe things that happen (Sc1);
- talk about what they saw (Sc1);
- start to make good guesses about outcomes (Sc1);
- make a record on a simple table consisting of two columns (Sc1);
- draw what they see (Sc1).

What have they experienced?

Children should have:
- carried out simple experiments under guidance;
- examined a variety of living things;
- handled a variety of materials;
- experienced a variety of pushes and pulls and other forces;
- examined a variety of sources of light and sound.

How have they made their knowledge public?

They should have:
- discussed their work with others;
- displayed their work through drawings, simple models, graphs and tables;
- written short sentences, with your help, where possible.

History

In the QCA's *Early learning goals* document, history is included in the category 'Knowledge and understanding of the world'. This section requires children to have some exposure to talking about their own lives and their families including past events.   In fact, reception children should be introduced to very little which could be separately identified as 'history' and it will rarely be of the familiar 'kings and queens and dates' variety.

What should they be able to do?

Reception children are at the beginning of their learning experiences and do not yet have sufficient knowledge of the world or of 'subjects' to cope with academic history. They can, however, begin the journey towards historical understanding. They are quite capable of learning about their environment, the people in it, and about features of the manufactured world including historic sites and objects.

Key areas

The door to history for very young children is opened by 'concrete' experiences (what they can see and touch) and the imagination (story and play). Hence teaching at this stage should focus on the following key areas:
- experiences of the world around;
- use of senses and powers of observation;
- exploratory play;
- talk – questioning and discussing;
- story.

You can expect the majority of children of this age to:
- begin to wonder about other people's lives as well as their own;
- ask questions about how people used to live in the past;
- begin to notice similarities and differences between then and now;
- begin to come to an imaginative understanding that a different past world existed;
- begin to acquire a basic 'time' vocabulary.

The greater the children's maturity, the wealth of their experiences and their ability to express thoughts, the greater will be their perceptiveness, observations and curiosity about the past.

Your expectations should not be too high. It is worth remembering, for example, that the language of time, its tenses and vocabulary, itself poses difficulties. Even 'yesterday' or 'tomorrow' can be a challenging concept as this example shows:

'It was my birthday', five-year-old Jason told me with a beaming smile.

'When was it, Jason?' ... *'Tomorrow, or the next week I think. I forgot.'*

Remember that in a child's development this is a preparatory stage for future history learning similar to being 'ready to read'. Although the child's understanding is undeveloped, we can still begin to lay the foundations for the time when this understanding matures.

Practical ideas

Making a start

The world around you

Plan to make use of the world around you by looking for potential historical opportunities in your school and in the locality. For example, school buildings themselves have a past and there may be plaques and memorials which commemorate founders or special events. Log books and registers can provide a story to link children's lives to the past.

Many new schools or local roads are named after events or people which link the past with the present and can provide starting points for discussion. Be sensitive to the historical dimension when considering people, places or things in other work at school. You don't need to drag history in at every opportunity, but it's as well to plan when you might include it or it will be overlooked.

Historical links

When tackling familiar topics such as 'Myself', 'Holidays' and 'People who help us', consider the history potential. For example, talk about the children's own past and invite them to bring in photographs of themselves 'then' and 'now'.

● Talk about events in the children's families to help them link the past with the present. Consider holidays, talk about holidays the children might have taken and ask: *Did mummy go for holidays when she was little? Where did she go?* Collect holiday postcards and talk about them.

● Relate events to other people who the children might know such as the school cleaner, and ask her to talk to the children about what life was like when she was at school.

● Keep each of these historical links, short and simple. Don't labour points or go into too much unnecessary detail which could put the children off and prevent them taking an interest next time you try to introduce some historical links.

Developing key areas

Observing

Children can be trained to use their senses and powers of observation. Encourage them simply to say what they see. Their comments will be honest and direct as they do not carry the weight

of experience and inhibition that adults do. These initial comments can be developed and built upon and the children's powers of observation can be developed using the ideas given here.

● Sit the children in a circle and pass round an appropriate historical artefact (for example a candle snuffer – make sure that it is something that can stand a good deal of handling). Ask each child to say something about the object if they can. Emphasise that they don't have to speak and repetition doesn't matter. You might expect to get comments such as 'It's cold.' 'It's metal.' 'It's pointy.' Ideally, spend five minutes a day doing this to improve the children's skills. The item could be anything – even a piece of chalk.

● Extend the above activity by including an adult in the circle to add more sophisticated comments. Pass the object round more than once and let talk develop. Encourage the children to give longer and more adventurous answers, even when these appear off-target.

● Children who have practised the object-passing activity can move on to a more focused interrogation of evidence. Use key question words such as *What? How? Who?* Try to shift the emphasis from the object to the people who may have used it. *What kind of person used this?* You can even raise gender issues. *Do you think it belonged to a man? Would a woman have used it?*

Then and now

● When using objects or visiting historical places (simply bigger objects!), try to match the 'then' with the 'now'. Compare a double earth closet (with a child's seat next to mother's) to a modern flush lavatory, for example. Use photographs where the object is not available (and even when it is). A photograph provides useful back-up and often some contextual clues as well.

● Although 'then' and 'now' are important key words, avoid precise dating ('When your Granny was four' may convey something to a child but '1938' means nothing.) 'Old' and 'new' are less useful as terms for several reasons, not least because the condition of the object can confuse the child. Focus on function and use comparing for example:

▶ flat iron versus an electric iron;
▶ wooden peg versus a plastic peg;
▶ enamel or china potty versus plastic potty;
▶ wooden play bricks versus plastic bricks;
▶ pocket watch versus modern wrist watch;
▶ Cod bottle (with a glass marble stopper) versus a soft drinks can.

Feeling and handling objects

● Make a mystery 'feely' box by placing a variety of items inside a box which children can investigate by touch alone. Let them put their hands inside and describe what they can feel. Start them off by asking for one word descriptions (hard, soft, long, thin). Then encourage them to develop their ideas into more detailed comments and perhaps even to guessing what the item is.

● Have an object table with one or two carefully chosen objects on. Encourage the children to handle them, take them apart, and talk about them (watch the safety angle). Add clues about the objects each day (a photograph; a word; a sentence of information; a relevant picture or story book). At the end of the week (or when appropriate) have a class discussion. Treat it as a detective activity. *Can we solve the mystery?*

Where to get objects

You may not need to buy anything at all to build up a school collection, it is surprising what you can gather from friends and colleagues. Consider jumble sales, car boot sales, the attic, the back of the stock cupboard and charity shops as sources of useful 'treasure'.

Borrow items whenever possible (check on the school insurance cover). Most areas have active County Museum and Library services which operate loan systems. At this stage avoid using reproductions as experience shows that they are not a cheap option and the notion of a reproduction is too sophisticated an idea for children of this age. They can be used with greater effect later on in the children's school careers.

Choosing objects

Provide a range of objects including:
▶ daily life objects which illustrate change in the domestic world (horseshoes; scrubbing brushes; clothes horses; carpet beaters);
▶ objects with a school connection (slates, sand trays, ink-wells, old books).

Don't forget that buildings and places are objects (although rather large ones), so you should treat them in a similar way to smaller artefacts (handing them round should be avoided). Look, interrogate and touch whenever possible.

History trail

● Make a school history trail. Even the newest buildings contain points that can be identified with 'then' as opposed to 'now'. In particular, look for: foundation stones and plaques; memorials; maps and pictures; date stones and old inscriptions (for example 'Boys entrance'); old fittings (old radiators, school bell, clock); furniture (blackboards, black and white televisions, BBC Master computers – from the old days).

● Walk the trail. Talk about it (of course!) and make labels and signs for the 'tourists'. Try numbering the stopping points on the trail and get different children to act as guides to other children making the tour.

● Let the class make a guidebook, including pictures, photographs, words and sentences about the trail.

● Use similar strategies on the school grounds and surrounding area, such as the High Street, or any suitable locality close by with which the children are familiar.

Visits

Any visits out of school to historic sites (if you decide to make them at all with this age group), must have a very specific focus. Choose one aspect of the site or one question to provide the focus of the trip; this might be *What?* or *Who?* Some teachers undertake visits to 'Victorian' school rooms with reception children but these may be of more value with older infants. Four-and five-year-olds do not yet have a 'now' school experience to compare with the 'then'.

Stories

Stories and imaginative approaches are powerful ways of coming to an understanding of the experiences of other people (whether in the past or not). Stories can often get over a lot of information in a short time and also help to extend the children's language.

● Tell stories from your own memory or imagination, without a book intervening. In this way you can control the pace and vocabulary to suit the children in your class.

● Share a book with the children rather than reading it to them as passive 'listeners'. Involve them in the story.

● Tell a story with another adult – swapping to tell the story from different viewpoints.

● Tell the story in role, but don't try to be too clever! A simple prop (hat or cloak) will often do the trick, especially if you can vary your voice to suit different characters. The children will respond to the fact that you are wearing your 'story-telling' shawl or coat and will know that when you put it on they are in for a treat.

● Create a story-telling corner where children can tell and re-tell stories to each other. Provide a prop box or use puppets and a puppet theatre. The line between story-telling and dressing-up for creative play is blurred for children. The distinction is unimportant as they will come to terms with new learning through both these activities, they will learn to sequence events in order, and begin to understand imaginatively what life was like in the past.

● Recreate favourite stories on storyboards. Discuss the story with the children, agree on the six or so main scenes in the story and then allocate the task of creating each part of the story to a group of children. This can be done visually (on a real board) or each group can act out their particular part of the storyboard.

● Set up some 'still life' scenes from stories with the children frozen in position. On a given word, they unfreeze and carry on the story until told to freeze again. You will need to rehearse a simple scene before they start so that they are all clear about 'what happens next'. Develop this using different groups, dressing-up clothes and so on.

Which stories?

Once upon a time there seemed to be no suitable history stories for very young children, yet all the while parents and teachers were telling 'Once upon a time', 'Long ago' and 'When I was a little girl' stories. Even these simple starter phrases are a beginning, part of an understanding that there were other times and places. In fact there is plenty of story material to choose from as long as you remain sensitive to the basic needs of the children.

● Unless you can establish some obvious link to the real world of your children (a national event, a local connection, a link with a TV programme) then you should not bother with straight historical stories about events or people. The story of Guy Fawkes may be an exception, although even this one poses problems (take out the violence, torture, religious intolerance and political intrigue and there is not much left for reception children). Powerful legends and mythical tales that are good stories in their own right may also have historical value, although that would not be your main reason for telling them.

● Simple stories which build an understanding that the past existed and provide a sense of a different era are the best kind to use and there are many infant stories that do this in some way. If you trawl through old reading schemes you will find many traditional tales, usually excellent readable versions, that fit the bill. Some of these stories may be explicitly historical (for example, 'Alfred and the cakes') but do not use them if the history aspect is laboured.

● The most important yardstick by which all the stories you use should be judged is *Is it a good story?*. The other element to look for is a connection, usually social, with the children's own experiences. Stories that involve different generations, especially stories about grandma and grandad, are particularly good as they provide a familiar family link as well as lots of 'then' and 'now' comparisons.

● If you check through the picture story books on your shelves you may be surprised to find how many books of this sort you already possess. As new books are coming on to the market all the time, the compilation of a definitive list is not possible but the examples quoted here will give you a good idea of what to look for.

The Story of a Castle, John S Goodall (Out of print).
Every picture tells a story, in this case the story of a castle from when it was first built to its life today as a tourist attraction. There are no words but the large sequenced illustrations are excellent. Do not use the book from cover to cover, but dip into it or use it on a picture a day basis.

Annabel's House, Norman Messenger (Out of print).
Another picture book that beautifully introduces children to every room in a large Edwardian house. Discreet but fun are the cut-out characters

house. Discreet but fun are the cut-out characters you can secrete around the 'house' to surprise the children. Doors and cupboards open to reveal their exciting contents. A high quality 'ooh...aah' book that is interactive, entertaining and informative.

My Great Grandpa, Martin Waddell and Dom Mansell (Walker Books).
Moving two generations away from the children is a good idea (so many grandparents are far too active these days to fit the traditional image) for the book features the declining physical powers of the elderly, as well as focusing on the understanding relationships that can form between the very young and the very old. As it touches lightly on concepts such as memory, change and growth, the book gradually reveals that Great Grandpa knows things (from the past) that nobody else knows.

Good Girl Granny, Pat Thomson and Faith Jaques (Victor Gollancz).
'Granny' books are, of course, equally useful from the history point of view. This one is sold as a 'share-a-story' book but is perfect reception history. 'In my day...' says granny searching for an example of behaviour to shame her grandchild, but what she comes up with are amusing and shocking incidents of misbehaviour from her youth. A storyline every child (and adult) will identify with.

When Grandma Was Very Young, Paul Humphrey and Katy Sleight (Evans).
Overtly didactic (the book compares now and then), nevertheless its simple direct approach is pitched at just the right level. 'What did people wear when you were young, grandma?' The answer is revealed on the facing page by photographs on a plain white background. 'When I was young people wore clothes like this.'

Wilfred Gordon McDonald Partridge, Mem Fox (Puffin).
A genuinely heart-warming tale about a little boy trying to find out what a memory is from the residents of an old people's home. Wilfred sets off on his quest when he hears his father say that his favourite resident, ninety-six year old Miss Nancy Alison Delacourt Cooper ('she had four names just as he did') had lost hers and he, being

her best friend, decides to find one for her. And he does.

From Me to You, Paul Rogers (Orchard Books).
This picture story book has become something of a classic. It is a tale being told by a grandma to her granddaughter about her life since 'coming into this world eighty years ago - inside all was lamps and firelight, outside was white with snow. Or so my mother told me. What does a baby know?' The thread running through the book (from me to you) is the lace-edged christening robe eventually turned into a handkerchief by grandma's own hands. It deals with legacy, generations and emotional links with the past.

And Miss Carter Wore Pink, Helen Bradley (Out of print).
When she was sixty, Helen Bradley began painting to illustrate her 'turn of the century' Lancashire childhood for her grandchildren. Her style, a cross between Grandma Moses and Lowry, is readily accessible to children. The powerfully evocative text (for adults) forms an excellent basis for teacher-child discussions about the events in Edwardian England that the pictures portray. The book contains many anecdotes for re-telling.

Assessment

Don't do it. Trying to assess four- and five-year-olds on their ability in this particular subject makes no sense, so you should concentrate on statutory baseline assessments.

In an informal way you can look for signs that the children are becoming aware of the world around them and forming an idea of 'then' and 'now'.

By the end of this year the children's powers of observations should have improved and through a variety of teaching methods they will have had the chance to extend their understanding.

You should, however, watch out for extremes of performance, identifying those children who are likely to require special needs provision as well as those who might be expected to accelerate quickly through the core curriculum. In either case, the information is valuable to parents and to yourself – but formal assessment in history comes later.

Geography

During the foundation stage and the early stages of Key Stage 1, children will be learning about places in general and about small localities starting with their local area. This will include the immediate vicinity of the school, including the school buildings, the grounds and surrounding area within easy access, probably within walking distance for the children. The children can compare this with contrasting localities of a similar size. They can learn about another part of their city, a locality in a nearby village, in a neighbouring town, or in 'natural' countryside. You may prefer to choose an overseas locality with which you yourself are familiar.

In the reception class you will be introducing children to the four key areas of geography:
- ability to undertake geographical enquiry and use geographical skills;
- knowledge and understanding of places;
- knowledge and understanding of geographical patterns and processes;
- knowledge and understanding of environmental change and sustainable development.

During the foundation stage, geography is taught under the umbrella of the area of learning entitled, 'Knowledge and understanding of the world'. The early learning goals are closely linked to the National Curriculum, and, as in all subjects, the early learning goals for children at the end of the foundation stage (the end of the reception year) are broadly equivalent to working at level one of the National Curriculum.

By working with the early learning goals and introducing the key areas of geography at Key Stage 1, the children in your reception class will be well-prepared for their geography work in the National Curriculum during Year One.

The emphasis of geography work in the reception class should be on providing spatial experiences in school and the immediate environment, helping children to acquire the language both to describe the environment and to talk about their experiences, and to begin to acquire graphicacy skills.

The early learning goals for most children at the end of the foundation stage in the areas of Knowledge and understanding of the world that are linked to geography are:
- to observe, find out about, and identify features in the place they live and the natural world;
- to begin to know about their own cultures and beliefs and those of other people;
- to find out about their environment, and talk about those features they like and dislike.

What should they be able to do?

In the reception class, children should begin to make progress in the four key areas of geography, listed below, which will be integrated in the activities you provide.

Key area: Geographical enquiry and skills

They should begin to:
● understand and use geographical vocabulary;
● respond to questions about places and environment topics on the basis of information you provide;
● make their own observations about places and environment from first-hand experience and secondary sources such as photographs;
● undertake simple tasks using and making maps, diagrams, photographs and other resources you provide, possibly initiated by play.

Key area: Knowledge and understanding of places

They should begin to:
● recognise and describe the main features of their local area, and any other localities they study, using appropriate geographical vocabulary;
● understand the significance of location, why features are where they are, why things happen where they do (for example: the location of shops; where puddles form in the playground);
● compare and contrast the localities they study and places they visit, recognising similarities and differences between them.

Key area: Knowledge and understanding of patterns and processes

They should respond to questions about:
● where things are (for example: maths equipment is kept together; classrooms are in a row along the corridor; most traffic goes along main roads);
● physical (natural) and human processes: why things are like they are (for example: there are puddles in the playground only when it rains; a new estate is being built because more people want to live here).

Key area: Knowledge and understanding of environmental change and sustainable development

They should begin to:
● express their own views about physical and/or human features of their environment (for example: *I like the classroom when it's quiet/tidy*);
● recognise that their environment changes and that people affect it (for example: *the classroom's tidier if we put things away in the right place*).

These aspects are looked at in more detail in Practical ideas on page 83, although the focus is on geographical skills and enquiry, the tools of geography. The other key areas are included *within* the ideas or activities.

Practical ideas

Developing key areas

Geographical vocabulary

As a school, you should plan geographical language development through the foundation stage, KS1 and beyond.

You are probably developing geographical vocabulary with your class without thinking of it as geography, since much of the language of geography at this stage is ordinary, everyday language. But there is also some special terminology. Give your children opportunities to learn geographical language and special terminology through direct experience, practical activities and fieldwork, from TV, pictures, stories, role play and games.

In the reception class these opportunities will often start with play. Use the activities and equipment in the classroom to lead into early geography.

● Plan to use the everyday language of:

❱ direction (for example, *right/left*, *up/down*, *forwards/backwards*, *straight on*, *round the corner*, *over/across*);

❱ location (for example, *here/there*, *near/far*, *next to*, *behind*, *in front*, *above/below*, *on/under*);

❱ scale and distance (for example, *big/small*, *long/short*, *close/far away*);

❱ quality, aesthetics (for example, *quiet/noisy*, *pretty/ugly*, *tidy/untidy*, *clean/dirty*).

Use this language whenever opportunities arise: in PE, walking around school (for example on the way to assembly) or the school grounds. Much of this language is also relevant to the mathematics curriculum.

● Play 'Where's teddy?' using a toy bear. Invite the children to place it *in* a box, *under* a chair, *above* their head, *on* the table, *next to* the LEGO and so on. Turn it into an I-Spy game. Ask the children to describe where you have placed or hidden teddy. Do this inside and outside the classroom. Introduce distance (*How far away is teddy?*) and direction.

● Introduce the names of:

❱ features in the natural or physical environment, including landscape (hill, mountain, beach); water in the environment (river, sea, canal, lake); weather (rain, wind, clouds, snow, storm). This

is essential language preparation for KS2;
‣ features in the built or human environment, including settlement, economic activities, jobs, journeys and transport.

● Make full use of opportunities to go for short walks around school, the school grounds, the neighbourhood and further afield.

● Reinforce all the geographical language development using flash-cards, word books and charts and by playing games with the children. Build up a geographical word bank; devote a regular part of Literacy Hour to geographical words and stories.

● Encourage the children to make quality/ aesthetic value judgements, and to express an opinion, about individual aspects of their own environment. This can include the classroom, pictures, videos, school grounds, use of materials (for clothing, building, toys). Help them to realise that they will not all have the same opinion; encourage them to justify or explain their likes and dislikes to each other. Reinforce their opinions by placing 'smiley' and other faces in the appropriate places.

● Through role play, encourage the children to act out geographical contexts associated with shopping, industry, agriculture, transport, holidays (for example: convert the home corner into a café, a bus or aeroplane; play at being a farmer, a builder; go on 'pretend' holidays).

● Develop their skills of:
Observation: Go for a walk to see landmarks and routes; take photographs of landmarks (houses, shops, street furniture, open spaces); distinguish between fixed (buildings) and moving (people, traffic) features.
Memory and recall: Can they remember and recognise photographs of what they saw? Draw pictures of landmarks; sort photographs into 'saw/didn't see'.
Sequencing: Can they sequence photographs of landmarks into the correct order? Can they sort them into 'seen on right/seen on left'.
Description: Acquire and use the geographical vocabulary to label or describe landmarks; describe the route taken in words, in drawings, in large maps.

● Build up a comprehensive collection of photographs of the local area, in all weathers, in all seasons, at different times of the day. Use this for recognition, matching, sorting, sequencing, talking activities. (It is very useful – and considerably cheaper – to have multiple sets of prints made at the time of processing.)

Geographical knowledge

Begin to develop the children's geographical general knowledge.

● They should begin to learn the names of towns, villages, cities, areas of countryside, countries, seas and oceans, rivers and mountains,

even if at this stage they have little conceptual understanding.

● Use opportunities to talk about, visit or look at pictures of places, or the sites themselves, of local significance: beauty spots, landmarks, special buildings, route ways, newsworthy events; national and international significance: sporting events and teams events; visits, visitors, topical events.

● Create opportunities to talk about places the children have visited/where their relatives live/ that they have seen on TV/encountered in stories. Locate these places on a globe, on appropriate simple maps (for example, PVC floor maps which can be written on with washable felt-tipped pen) and in pictures.

● Encourage the children to contribute to vocabulary lists for these categories. Some of these lists will be universal (for example, weather) but to some extent they will be specific to your school, referring to the physical and human features in your local area and your chosen contrasting locality, including the features which give these places their particular character.

Geographical enquiry

Initially, you will be posing questions yourself for the children to respond to, while encouraging them to ask their own.

● Ask questions about places, about parts of the school and its grounds, about a visit, a story, a picture or a television programme, to encourage children's geographical thinking to extend beyond 'observe and describe'. For example: *What is it? What is it like?* (skill or concept: observation, description); *What sort of place is it?* (categorisation, classification); *Is it like any other places you know?* (comparison); *Where is it?* (location).

If it is a place the children have visited, or you are planning to visit:
How did/can/will we get there? (distance, direction, journey); *What do you feel about it? Do you like it?* (opinion, values, attitude) and if there is a problem, or something about the place the children don't like: *What can you do about it?* (action).

● Use photographs to ask different types of question. For example, using a photograph of people in a shopping mall you might ask: *What can you see?* (concrete); *What are the people doing?* (descriptive); *What would they do if it started to rain?* (speculative); *Why aren't the people wearing jumpers?* (reasoning); *Is this a good place to shop?* (evaluative); *How or where else could all these people do their shopping?* (problem-solving).

● Carry out a local geographical enquiry:

1 What can we buy in our local shops?

Observe: Visit and look at a local row of shops.
Ask questions: *How many shops are there? What can you buy in these shops? What type of shops are they? Are they all different types?*
Collect and record information: draw pictures, take photographs, collect samples.
Communicate information and ideas: make, and talk about, a class wall picture; sequence, label and talk about the photographs; locate photographs on a large scale wall map; make and talk about a display of samples; make and talk about a model of the row of shops.

2 What do people do in school?

Observe: Walk around school.
Ask questions: *Can you see any people? Where are they? What are they doing? Are they all doing the same thing? Do they do this all day long? Could they do it somewhere else?*
Collect and record information: draw pictures, take photographs, collect examples of what people are doing.
Communicate information and ideas: make, and talk about, a class wall picture; sequence, label and talk about the photographs; make and talk about a display of examples; make and talk about a model or plan of the school, locating the people on it.

Graphicacy skills

Graphicacy, 'the essentially pictorial communication of spatial information', has been described as 'the fourth ace in the pack', alongside literacy, oracy (articulacy) and numeracy. Geographers think it is possibly as important, as a life skill, to be graphicate as to be literate, articulate and numerate.

● Plan to introduce your children to graphicacy skills for:
❱ acquiring spatial information, including way-finding, using pictures, photographs; diagrams, aerial photographs, maps, plans, globes and atlases;
❱ giving spatial information, including making pictures and diagrams, making maps and plans.

Way finding

● Way-find around school, school grounds, and the local area/neighbourhood.

● Go for walks for first-hand experience; follow sign-posts positioned around school.

● Use figures/dolls on a large model/plan of the school (perhaps made for your class by older pupils). A map painted on an old bed sheet is useful and easily stored.

● Describe a walk to the children, using geographical vocabulary, encourage them to visualise and draw it.

Photographs

● Use pictures and photographs of the school, the school grounds, and the local area/ neighbourhood.

● Describe; match (play Snap with multiple copies of photographs); sequence; locate on a large model/plan.

● Make and use your own videos of school and the local area (you could enlist a parent's help) to remind children what they have seen, to talk about, to stop the tape and ask, for example, what occurs next or round the corner.

Using different perspectives

● Take photographs of buildings and features from the school rooftop or a neighbouring tall building (church tower, car park, block of flats); children can match them to photographs of the same features taken from ground level; talk together about where they are in relation to the classroom.

• Build up a collection of picture postcards taken from different perspectives, including oblique aerial views; talk about 'where the photographer was' to take the picture.

• Take photographs of classroom and school features from different perspectives (ground level, eye level, standing on a chair, from an upstairs window) for the children to sort and match.

• Use a video camera to film the class from above (top of a step ladder). A helpful parent might do this for you. Can the children identify themselves and classroom features?

Maps, plans, globes, atlases

• Use PVC floor maps (you can write on these with washable felt-tipped pens) to locate topical and familial places.

• Use play mats (although these often have a strange perspective) with different sized toy vehicles and so on – ask the children which is the most suitable size, and why.

• Play ball with inflatable globes; recognise land and sea.

• Provide picture atlases in the book corner.

Make pictures, diagrams, maps and plans

• Use familiar classroom equipment to progress from play into early graphicacy work.

• Encourage children to follow the assembly diagrams that accompany LEGO and other construction kits, thus interpreting 2D representations of 3D structures.

• Use the train set: start with free play, then create a plan of their layout by drawing round the track (1:1 scale); ask another child to reconstruct the layout from the 1:1 plan. Encourage children to record their layouts in picture and later in map form. Give them increasingly complex layout plans to construct. Take photographs of different layouts for the children to select and make. Take photographs of a few layouts from different perspectives (side view, oblique and vertical) for the children to sort (grouping together all the pictures which show the same layout).

• Use the sand tray: give children experience of a range of different materials either separately or mixed together. Use builders' aggregate, dried peas, rice, beach sand (mixed grain sizes, including pebbles), 'growbag' compost and so on. Start with free play; then encourage the children to create landscapes – a hill, a mountain, an island; then add features to the landscape – hedges, trees, roads, buildings (perhaps using LEGO).

Encourage them to record their landscape in picture and later in map form. *What happens when it rains* (use a watering can) *on the mountain? What happens when you try to create the sea round an island? Can you make cliffs, caves?*

• Use farm and zoo animals: start with free play, then encourage the children to use sugar paper and crayon (or chalk) to make a farm layout, their own 'play mat' showing fields or enclosures, roads and paths. Add buildings (LEGO for example). *Are the fields the same all through the year? Do all animals live in similar places, need the same things?* Introduce ideas about weather, seasons, harvest, use of flat and hilly land.

With the three ideas above, the children's early attempts at map-making will be very simple (disconnected circular fields, for example) and they will need repeated opportunities to develop their graphicacy skills.

• Record fieldwork – walks and journeys made by the class, around school, in the local area – in a variety of pictorial forms from large scale, wall display to individual drawings. Early attempts will probably be 'linear', telling the story of the walk; subsequent attempts will be 'circular', spatially more accurate in that they start and finish at the same place.

• Model the classroom – start with play, creating imagined rooms using boxes or bricks painted to represent furniture; use the 'furniture' boxes to model the classroom; place 'furniture' on an outline plan of the classroom (painted on an old bed sheet); encourage children to identify classroom features on the model, record representation in pictorial forms; record as plans.

• Encourage children to visualise stories spatially, to construct or expand them spatially, or represent

them as pictorial maps. *Where was the bridge where the troll lived – in a field? On a road? Was the bridge across a stream or a river? How deep was the water? Were there hills near the bridge?*

Weather recording

Start with play and talk; have a collection of clothes and accessories for children to dress a doll or teddy appropriately for that day's weather; record the clothes teddy wears. Let children invent their own symbols for recording daily weather before you introduce conventional weather symbols. Keep a weekly chart and talk about it at the end of the week; compare one week with the previous week.

Use ICT

Introduce children to *My World:* – 'Weather' and 'Make a town' which are both suitable geographical programs.

Use a concept keyboard with geographical overlays: photographs of the classroom and the school, an aerial photograph, and a simple map of the school grounds for the children to enter simple captions, likes and dislikes.

Assessment

At this stage you could keep simple records throughout the year to show the children's progress.

What do they know?

Consider how the children can use geographical vocabulary accurately and appropriately.

What can they do?

Assess their ability to way-find around school, their use of geographical skills, ability to ask and respond to geographical questions.

What have they experienced?

They should have had exposure to topics, activities and fieldwork (experiences outside the classroom).

How have they demonstrated their knowledge?

Evidence that the children have been successful will be apparent through their talk, drawing and practical activities such as sorting, matching and sequencing.

Music

During the foundation stage, the curriculum area of music is found in the area of learning entitled, 'Creative development', as outlined in the QCA document *Early learning goals*. The document explains that creativity is fundamental to successful learning. It recommends that children should be provided with a broad range of musical opportunities from singing simple songs from memory and responding to what is heard in a variety of ways (including matching movements to music), to expressing and communicating ideas, thoughts and feelings through a variety of songs and musical instruments.

These are very broad guidelines and give wide scope for an enthusiastic teacher whether musical or not, to explore sounds with all of the children in the reception class. You do not need to be a music specialist to introduce the musical elements of high, low, loud, soft, long, short, fast, slow, one sound, two sounds to all children in a variety of exciting ways. Many activities taking place in the reception class will include elements of 'music' particularly during song sessions, storytime, dance, music with movement and on listening walks.

Exploration of 'sounds' through the elements of music in the reception class can lead to a far greater understanding as they enter Key Stage 1.

Key areas: Listening, composing, performing, appraising

A curriculum for music-making will always ask for sounds to be explored through listening, composing, performing, appraising and at times it is useful to look at the areas separately. However, in a successful music session all four areas are in action at the same time. A music maker will listen to sounds, discuss them, choose appropriate ones to place together in some order, move them around and then perform them. This is no less true in a reception class than it is at University level and should be encouraged at all times.

These skills are involved in all the activities suggested in this chapter which explore seven key elements of music. These are: *pitch* (high/low), *duration* (long/short), *dynamics* (loud/

quiet/silence), *tempo* (fast/slow), *timbre* (tinkling/rattling/smooth/ringing sounds), *texture* one or more sounds) and *structure* (building a piece of music).

Sometimes in spite of being enjoyable, a music session can lack purpose. For example: *Let's have a sing song ... Shall we play on the instruments? ... Now dance to this music ...* Make the sessions more focused, interesting and effective by being aware of the musical elements and directing the activities towards their exploration.

What should they be able to do?

Key element: Pitch

Pitch simply means whether or not a sound is high or low. Of course there are sounds in between and sounds can be made to slide up or down and it is all these variations that you will be inviting the children to explore.

The most important activity in which to involve children who are making music is listening. Some children may have actively listened for different sounds with their parents or at nursery, but most will find it a novel activity. Most will not naturally listen for specific sounds but, once encouraged, will find it great fun.

We live in a noisy world of voices, traffic sounds, banging doors, overhead planes, building site sounds, *musak*, blaring televisions and radios, and children accept all this as background noise. Encourage them to identify differences in sounds and to recognise them.

They will not naturally know which sounds are high or which sounds are low and so need to learn by experience. If by the end of the year they can recognise the difference, this will create a sound base for other teachers to work with later on in school.

Key element: Duration

Duration in music means long or short and can be described as a pulse or a rhythm. From a very early age children tap out sounds banging irregular noises on the side of a cot, shaking a toy or banging a drum. These are all long and short sounds. Once those random sounds become more regular, they can be called a pulse or rhythm.

At this stage of experimenting, it is enough for you to listen with the children to a great many sounds and to decide whether they are long or short.

They will enjoy experimenting with their voices and with a few untuned percussion instruments – cymbals (long), blocks (short), triangles (long/short), tambourines (long/short) – to see how long or short they can make the sounds. By the end of the year they should be able to do this effectively.

Key element: Dynamics

Dynamics in music means loud/quiet/silence/getting louder/getting softer. Children are usually very responsive when asked to make a loud sound but find quiet and silence more difficult. Exploring dynamics creates a good opportunity to establish some rules about how important it is to have silences in music. Let the children copy you creating loud or soft sounds to give them a guide as to how loud or how soft a sound can be. Give them also the opportunity just to be silent.

By the end of the year, most children should be able to use some instruments and their voices in a quiet way, be able to make louder sounds in a controlled way and be responding to silence.

For some of the games suggested (Hunt the thimble, page 98), children will be asked to create sounds that get louder and softer. This is more difficult, but many children will be able to do it in quite a controlled way and everyone should be encouraged to try. Young children will know what 'loud' and 'soft' mean but in music-making the aim is to control these sounds.

Key element: Tempo

Fast/slow is tempo in music-making. First of all you will need to decide what is normal and then agree to get faster or slower.

To begin with, you can expect many children to rush ahead of you whether you are clapping or tapping a simple beat. Have patience until there is a feel of unity in the sound, then gradually get slower before getting faster. Trying to march together can be fun and quite a challenge to keep the beat of the feet steady. Quieter-sounding instruments, such as bells, played by all the children can also be used to keep a beat and then to change it, creating a very pleasing sound. By the end of the year, a beat should be held by all with some acceptable changes of pace.

Key element: Timbre

The timbre of music is the quality of the sound. At the beginning of the year, most children will just hear sounds, general background sounds, but nothing specific. Gradually, with practice, they will identify loud, soft, short, long, high and low sounds. Timbre is a much more subtle concept involving such variations as tinkling, rustling or scraping; it is the very special individual sound that each thing makes and children will need to be shown these subtle differences.

A useful starting point for young children in their understanding of timbre, is that everyone's voice has a different sound. By listening to different voices, children can also learn to recognise different sounds.

Body percussion creates different kinds of sounds: claps are not like clicks or stamps. We use them in music-making to create different effects.

Every instrument will also have a voice of its own and, by the end of the year, most children can be expected to recognise the sound of the well-known untuned percussion instruments.

Key element: Texture

The texture of music refers to there being one sound or more. All young children like to sing songs, sometimes on their own and sometimes with others. A solo has one sound while a choir has quite a different sound; they have different textures. The same applies to instruments: one instrument played on its own creates one texture but a school band or an orchestra has quite another texture.

Texture is a difficult concept for very young children to understand but by the end of a year, they should be hearing the differences between a solo voice/instrument and a small group of singers/players.

Key element: Structure

All the elements of music encourage exploration of sounds but it is exciting to put some of these elements together in an organised way and this is the musical structure. It can be as simple as a repeated spoken or sung phrase that gets louder and then softer. The phrase 'Train is on its way' can be sung on any one note chosen by a child beginning softly, getting louder, becoming very loud and then disappearing into the distance until there is silence. This exercise demonstrates a beginning, a middle and an end and that is its structure.

Children's songs and nursery rhymes are often based on repeated words and this creates their easy to remember structure. Poetry, which has repeated phrases as a chorus, also encourages the idea of a need for structure and can be sung or have its rhythm played.

By the end of the year, children will have naturally experienced many different structures since many of the rhymes sung will have a structure. For example, there is a question and answer in the song '1, 2, 3, 4, 5, Once I Caught a Fish Alive', repetition in 'I Am the Music Man', and all stories to musical accompaniments will have a beginning, a middle and an end.

An awareness of these seven elements of music should make for some exciting explorations of sounds.

Practical ideas

The easiest way to involve all the children in musical activities is to make sure you can see them and they can see you. Sit them in a circle around you whenever possible, insist on silence while you give your instructions and make sure you have eye contact with them all. Keep the activities short and change them frequently, alternating a listening activity with a movement activity whenever possible.

Making a start

Sing a song

Choose a song you know very well such as 'The Animals Went in Two by Two', 'Five Little Speckled Frogs' or 'The Wheels on the Bus'. Sing the whole song through a couple of times for the children to enjoy and get the feel of the sound. Now sing a line, making sure all the children listen, then ask the children to sing it with you, and then sing another line. Use this pattern to teach all new songs.

Hello song

Name games are always popular and for children in the reception class they are also an important part of getting to know new friends. Create a 'Hello song' to the tune of a well-known song or rhyme to suit your own group of children. Here is one to the tune of 'Shalom My Friends' (*Flying a Round*, A&C Black):

Hello to Jane and Mark and Lee,
There's Rav-in-der too,
Hello to Salma, Ewan and James,
I'll clap the names with you.

Everyone will want their name to be included, so the song will have to be adapted. Ask the children to clap the names with you; some names will need one clap, some two, a few will need three or more.

Clap and copy

A good starter activity is to clap and ask the children to copy you. Keep it steady and then gradually get slower before getting faster again. Try to encourage the children not to make the sound louder as they get faster; it is very hard to do. Try the same idea with some instruments, although the result could be very noisy!

Instruments

● Gather together a collection of as many different-sounding, untuned percussion instruments as possible. Include triangles, tambourines, castanets, drums, rain-maker, cabasa, agogo bells and wood blocks. Place a few of the instruments in the centre of the circle to be used, when needed, by just a few of the children. Demonstrate a sound with one of the instruments and invite a child to copy you. As the children get more used to the instruments you can gradually work towards everyone having one to make specific sounds, with silences between.

● Show the children how to hold the instruments correctly. A good way to begin is to mime the playing of instruments in 'I Am the Music Man'.

Listening

● Take the children on a listening walk as a good starting point. Either make your walk around the school and grounds or if possible venture out on a short walk in the immediate vicinity of the school. Encourage the children to listen to the many noises. *What can you hear? Can you name some of the things which you can clearly hear?* On the first listening walk collect sounds and talk about them later in the classroom.

Make a second listening walk to listen for high/ low sounds, short/ long sounds, loud/ quiet sounds and those which get louder and softer. Back in the classroom talk about what you have heard. Try to find or draw pictures to show the objects making the sounds which you heard and make charts to show what you heard and where.

● Listen through an open window for sounds that are loud/ soft/ get louder or softer. Ask the children to listen to the sounds of footsteps coming towards or away from them and talk about how the sounds change.

Introducing key elements

Voices

● One of the most effective ways of teaching children about the musical elements is to play 'Copy me'. Use the idea of the game 'Simon says' to get high, low, long, short, loud, soft and silent responses.

● Ask the children to close their eyes, then touch one child to say an agreed phrase. *Who is speaking?* Can the children recognise the timbre of the voice? Then ask the chosen speakers to respond in a high or low voice. Can everyone still recognise who is speaking?

● Listen to voices to hear if some sound higher or lower than others. Sing songs in high voices and then low voices. Use well-known stories to demonstrate high/low voices for the various characters (such as Goldilocks, Red Riding Hood or the Three Little Pigs).

● The voice is a good instrument to use to explore long and short sounds. It is readily available and can be made to do all kinds of things. Pass long vocal sounds around a circle with each child waiting until the previous child's sound has disappeared. Short vocal sounds are passed around much faster.

● Simple rounds, when one voice begins and is joined by another and then another, creates a different texture. Children in reception find it difficult to take part in round-singing unless the song is very simple and both groups are led by adults. As an alternative to singing rounds themselves, let the children listen to an older group of children singing to appreciate the textures which are created.

● Ask the children to try to recreate sounds they have heard with their voices. Most of them will already be familiar with the idea of recreating animal sounds with their voices and some of them

will be expert at doing other sounds such as police car sirens! They can also try to recreate the sounds with untuned percussion.

Body percussion

● Encourage the children to use their bodies as instruments. Clapping, knee slapping, finger clicking and foot stamping all make good sounds.

● Many of the action songs suitable for this age range involve clapping hands, stamping feet, clicking fingers or slapping knees. This is all body percussion and the children can add different sounds on sounds. *Okki-tokki-unga* (A&C Black), is a useful collection of action songs.

● Use the body as an instrument to make short sounds as well as fast and slow sounds and to explore new sounds.

Instruments

● Put a collection of untuned percussion instruments (triangle, wood block, tambourine, castanets, rain-maker and guiro) in the centre of a circle of children. Pick out one instrument and play it. Ask the children to help you decide if the sounds played are long or short or maybe both. Put the instruments in groups.

● On another occasion discover how to play the instruments quietly as well as loudly.

● If the instruments are played singly, then two together, then three, the sounds produced will create new textures. If you can play guitar or piano to accompany the children's singing you will be able to create another texture. Experiment with the children to find new and interesting combinations of sounds.

● Instruments also have their own timbre and it can be fun trying to recognise them. Hide a few instruments inside a large cardboard box, and invite one child to go into the box and play one. Ask the other children to listen and decide which of the instruments is making the sound they can hear.

● Introduce instruments from other countries and cultures to the children if you can. Ask parents and friends to bring them into music sessions to demonstrate to the children.

● Encourage rhythm in dance and movement sessions, as the children react to the rhythmic sounds of taped music, the beat of a tambourine, the click of the castanets or the longer sounds of the gong and the rain-maker played in a repeated pattern. Ask them to listen to a steady beat on the tambourine, then to push the air with their hands in front of them one at a time. Change to shaking the tambourine. *How will your movements change?* Use both in a sequence and invite the children to react. Develop this idea using feet as well as hands.

Developing key elements

Using the voice

Sing with the children, at every opportunity. If you are a confident singer, let the children copy you as you sing new songs. If you prefer some help, find good recordings of appropriate songs to use. (The Early Learning Centre has some excellent tapes.)

Repetition is the key to success at this stage, find the children's favourite songs and keep singing them at every opportunity. Combining actions with songs often helps children to learn and remember them, so whenever possible add appropriate movements. Always encourage shy children to join in with you, ask a best friend to sing along with them or place them next to a confident singer. Discourage shouters by asking them to listen to others and then to join in again. Everyone can sing, some people just need more practice than others.

Making up songs

● Sit in a circle and, to the tune of 'Polly Put the Kettle On', sing this song pointing to the children as their name occurs. You could change your seat so that the name of the person sitting next to you changes. The names could also be clapped, first by you and then by the children:
Ronan's sitting next to Jack
Iqbal's sitting next to Anne
Kwai Ling's sitting next to Tom
Who's sitting next to me?

● Children like familiar tunes, so together make up some short songs to well-known tunes. You could invent a song called 'High and Low' to the

Music

tune of 'Pease Pudding Hot', beginning, *I can point high, I can point low...* and add some movements.

● To the tune of 'Postman Pat' write words beginning: *Soft and loud, Soft and loud, Let us all clap...* and so on.

● Ask the children which is their favourite movement (jumping, running or hopping). To the tune of 'Here We Go Round the Mulberry Bush' create an action song, like this:
My friend Fatima likes to dance, likes to dance, likes to dance
My friend Fatima likes to dance so dance along with me.
My friend Christopher likes to jump....
My friend Winston he likes to hop....
My friend Chloe she likes to run....
The book *Bobby Shaftoe Clap Your Hands* (A&C Black) has lots of suggestions for creating action songs to well-known tunes.

Listen together

Sometimes it's a good idea just to listen to music without singing, without moving and without dancing. Choose short pieces which encourage the children to use their imagination while they listen, such as Prokofiev's 'Peter and the Wolf' or 'Tubby the Tuba'.

Listen to these pieces just as stories with music. At this stage it is not important for the children to know what a clarinet or bassoon look like – only that the clarinet makes a good 'cat' sound or that the bassoon's low notes sound like a prowling wolf. These initial listening sessions may lead to some drama and dance, but it's important to start with simply listening.

Divide Saint Saen's 'Carnival of the Animals' into short listening sessions and this could easily lead to drawing and painting activities as well as dance and movement.

Body percussion

Ask the children to copy you as you clap your hands four times. They will try to anticipate your action, make sure they listen and watch quietly. Repeat the action, change the number of claps, move to finger clicking, then foot tapping and knee slapping. Keep the actions as simple as possible. Some songs such as 'If you're happy and you know it' and 'First you make your fingers

click' (*Flying a Round*, A&C Black) encourage specific actions.

Instruments

● Ask each child to choose a favourite instrument and talk about it to the other children. Encourage them to say why they have chosen that instrument. *Is it the colour, the size, the shape, the sounds it can make? How many sounds can you make on it? Which other instruments might sound good if they were played with it? How does it make you feel when you hear it?*

● Make a collection of items such as squeezy bottles, small pieces of wood, yoghurt cartons, foil, string, plant pots, a bucket, metal spoons, cotton reels, seeds and other found objects. Provide a supply of glue, rubber bands and Sellotape. See if the children can devise ways of making their own instruments which resemble real instruments. Ask them to look carefully at the real instrument first to find out how the sounds are made before making their own version.

● All instruments can be played loudly or softly but different playing techniques can also change the sounds produced. Let the children explore possible sounds with you. Try holding a beater closer to an instrument to produce a softer sound, exerting less pressure. Shake or play an instrument more vigorously for a louder sound. A tambourine can be shaken, hit or scraped and each sound is a new timbre.

Experiment with the children to find how many instruments you can shake, rattle or ring, then use these techniques to describe characters in stories or use them in a movement session.

● Invite parents/friends who play an instrument to visit the class and play their instrument for the children. Encourage them to talk to the children about their instrument and perhaps join in the class music-making.

Dancing music

Children enjoy responding to music through dance and this is to be encouraged. It is a great asset if you can play the piano or have access to a piano and a pianist to accompany the children. They can then have the opportunity to dance to the high or low, long or short, loud or soft sounds

as the pianist changes them, responding to the mood of the music.

Low, heavy sounds can invite the children to attempt elephant movements, while high, short, tinkling sounds might suggest leaves waving in the breeze. A monkey climbing a tree could be a response to low-to-high sounds and crashing chords might be a lion roaring through the jungle.

● However, if you have neither piano nor pianist you will have to rely on recorded pieces. Here are some suggestions which many children will already know, and to which they can respond in dance to the mood of the music. These examples are all from well-known films:

Mary Poppins – 'Jolly Holiday' (happy); 'Feed the Birds' (thoughtful); 'Step in Time' (rhythmic); 'Fly a Kite' (contented); 'One Man Band' (lively).
Jungle Book – 'Colonel's March'; 'Trust in Me'.
Wizard of Oz – 'Over the Rainbow'.
Lady and the Tramp – 'Siamese Dance'.
Winnie the Pooh – 'Up, Down, Touch the Ground'.
The Lion King – 'I Want to be King'.
Aladdin – 'Whole New World'.

The music can be used in a variety of ways and can generate quite a lot of discussion. *Listen to this piece of music? Do you know this song? Can you join in? Has anyone seen this film? How does the music make you feel? Sad? Happy? Lazy? Grumpy? Why? When I play the music again, I want you to stand up and move first your head to the music, then your arms, then your feet. Next time move round the room dancing to the song.*

Animal music

Invite the children to tell you about their favourite animals. *What sounds do they make?* Ask them to create similar sounds with their voices. Can they recreate any of the sounds on instruments? (Bird songs on whistles/ recorders, cuckoo on xylophone, lamb bleats by shaking a tambourine, frog by scraping the guiro, wood blocks as horse hooves.)

Sit in a circle and ask each child to create one animal sound. Listen to each one, and then tell them to watch you carefully as you are the conductor. Point randomly to different children to make their sound and see how quickly they respond. To complete the activity have fun with everyone joining in your 'Animal choir'.

Music and stories

Once the children are familiar with a story, storytime lends itself to music-making accompaniments. Look out for stories with repeated activities such as walking, running, jumping, climbing, hopping, flying or diving. Using just a few instruments, decide with the children how to represent different actions. For example: walking (wood block), running

Music

(tambourine), jumping (castanets), sliding (swanee whistle), hopping (agogo), flying (maracas). As the story is retold, invite some children to respond with their instruments. (*I wish I could fly* by Ron Maris (Julia MacRae Books) is an easy, enjoyable book for the children to accompany with music.)

They can also respond to stories with their voices (animal sounds, traffic noises, wind howling) and body percussion (knee slapping or toe tapping for raindrops, using their feet for running or walking sounds).

Ideas bank

Follow the sounds

Gather the children to sit in a circle with one child standing in the centre with eyes closed or blindfolded. Give one of the seated children some handbells. The child in the centre must listen to the bells being passed round behind the backs of the children in the circle. The child can shout 'Stop!' at any time and must point to the child he or she thinks is playing the bells. If the guess is right he or she joins the seated circle and the other child goes into the centre to listen.

Play sound games based on 'Hunt the thimble' using instruments, voices or hand clapping with louder or softer sounds to lead a child to a hidden object.

Listening bingo

Make a recording of twenty easily-recognised sounds (doors banging, bells ringing, birds singing, vacuum cleaner, lawn mower,

handclapping and so on). Find pictures in magazines and catalogues of the objects making sounds, and cut these out. (It may be easier to find the pictures first and then record sounds to match.)

Give pairs of children different pictures and an A5 size piece of card divided into six squares. Ask them to glue the pictures onto the card, one on each square. Now play Listening bingo – play the tape and, when the children hear a sound which matches with a picture on their card, they must cover the picture. Although the game takes time to prepare, it can be used with future classes. It may be possible to ask a helpful parent to make the tape and prepare the cards.

Unusual instruments

Involve the children in making a collection of everyday objects that will make interesting sounds (wood, tins, shells, sand or pebbles or rice in containers) and use them as instruments.

Sing a jingle

Most children will be familiar with television programmes for pre-school children. Encourage them to sing the jingles they have heard and, working with them, use the tunes to make up simple action songs. Add some percussion and perform the songs as part of a class assembly.

Sound quiz

If children have access to a tape recorder at home, ask their parents or carers to help them make a tape of different sounds. Listen to the tapes in school and see how many sounds the class can recognise.

Assessment

The most important outcome of music-making with children in the reception class is that they should enjoy it. This will be obvious at the end of the music session because they will want to sing, dance, clap, move, on the way to their next activity.

However it is also possible for you to evaluate whether or not you have achieved what you set out to do. The most important things for you to do in making music are to:
- get the children involved, encourage them to listen;
- get them to perform, ask them what they think;
- provide opportunities to create musical sounds and to put them together.

What can they do?

Use this checklist to see what they have learned.
Can they:
- Listen attentively to sounds?
- Collect sounds?
- Recognise some differences of sounds?
- Recreate sounds?
- Use sounds?
- Respond to sounds?
- Discuss sounds?

Music

What have they experienced?

Have they:

- Explored sounds both vocal and instrumental?
- Used their body as an instrument to make sounds?
- Handled and used some percussion instruments?
- Responded to music through dance and movement?

Can they perform?

Whenever possible, the children should be encouraged to perform. A class assembly, presented to other children, is a good opportunity for this.

The music-making should be shared as often as possible with other groups of children, parents and friends. At this stage, the best way is to invite parents, carers, friends and visiting music teachers to join in a music session and to make music together.

Art

For children in a reception class, learning about art is most naturally achieved through touching, handling and manipulating materials. Given any kind of drawing tool, or wet sand and a stick, most young children will make marks, given clay or dough, they will shape it into various forms and they enjoy the tactile and visual qualities of paint. Young children are naturally curious about everything, they are observant and will notice details. Their innate sense of wonder makes them ready to investigate whatever artistic methods you can provide.

The document *Early learning goals* (QCA) suggests in its 'Creative Development' section that children's experiences should include: exploring colour, texture, shape, form and space in two and three dimensions; responding to the senses in a variety of ways; using imagination in art and design and expressing and communicating ideas, thoughts and feelings by using a widening range of materials and tools. These activities link naturally to the suggestions for Art in the Key Stage 1 Programme of Study in the National Curriculum.

At this stage, your role is to encourage children to look, touch and then to have confidence in their own responses; to provide materials which enable them to explore and develop; to observe the ways in which they work and to show them a variety of ways in which tools and materials can be used.

What should they be able to do?

On entering reception, some children will have been stimulated to think and do, will have had access to good quality materials and will know how to use and respect them. Others, having had little or no previous experience, may not even know how to hold a drawing tool. This diversity challenges us from the start to respect the unique response which each child brings to art, and to find ways of providing appropriate experiences for all children.

Art

In the early stages you should have no preconceived ideas about what individual children will be able to do. They can only contribute what their emotional, intellectual and perceptual development will allow them to do but with challenges to respond, to wonder and explore, surprising things can happen.

Some children will not draw in the conventional sense. For most children in the reception class, experience is still based largely on kinaesthetic response. This means that you will see children's pleasure in the repeated movement of the pencil, crayon or brush over paper; the results are abstract scribble and pattern. The marks made will become increasingly more deliberate so that it becomes possible to see a repeated range of marks and shapes and relate them to recognisable things.

Pleasure will be experienced in the repeated movement of a pencil.

At this stage repetition is important, with children repeating experiences and ideas, going over the same thing again and again until the idea is mastered, sometimes with the addition of newly-understood variations and details. These shapes which children are able to repeat when needed are called 'schema'. Many of the children will have developed a schema for the human form, which is often the first to develop. The complexity of what they can produce will vary according to their experiences at home, playgroup or nursery school, and to their general ability and personal experiences. You will notice that children will begin to name some of their drawings and a personal symbolism, or collection of images, is built up. Images made with paint, and particularly those made using three dimensional materials, are usually less detailed than children's drawn imagery but can often express emotive and feeling responses.

Activities presented to children at this stage should be lively and enjoyable and are often spontaneous. Your aim as their teacher is to make children open to:

● look, touch, feel and ask questions;

● use and respond to tools and materials, to learn how to use them effectively and to care for them;

● have confidence to make their own responses and decisions;

● respond to the elements of art: line, tone, shape, form, colour, pattern, texture (which are the building blocks of art);

● respond to and talk about their own work and ideas;

● look at other people's paintings, drawings, models and patterns from all times and places.

Practical ideas

For practical reasons (such as limited materials, the potentially messy nature of the activity and carpeted areas where wet materials may not be used) art activities are usually best carried out in small groups. You should not see this as a reason for you to leave children to their own devices as your interaction with them is important for establishing appropriate language to describe the activity and to offer praise and encouragement. It is up to you to enable the children to work at a level where they can learn to appreciate colours, shapes, lines and patterns, through initial focused questioning and subsequent interaction and encouragement. Use encouragement such as: *What a lovely bright colour! Can you see another bright colour? What a lovely pattern you have made! Can you make a pattern with circles? Can you make a pattern using red and yellow? I like the wiggly lines you have painted. Can you paint some thick/straight/thin lines?*

Where possible, make use of help from any willing adults such as teaching assistants who could work with a group of children. Brief any helpers beforehand to make sure they understand both the children's developmental stage in art and the desired outcomes of the activity.

Teaching assistants and other adults should also understand the importance of accepting children's exploratory work, personal symbolism and imagery or visually real approaches with equal respect as they are all part of the developmental pattern. Consider involving parents, too, by keeping them informed and made welcome to come into the classroom and encouraging them to play a significant role in supporting learning opportunities in the classroom.

Making a start
A well-organised environment
A rich stimulating environment is essential if the children are to produce interesting artwork. Whenever possible, let the children work from real things as sensory learning is of paramount importance and the children will benefit from every possible opportunity for first-hand experience.

● Provide collections of all kinds in the classroom, encouraging children to contribute suitable items themselves. Consider making collections of: seasonal things (leaves, conkers), plants, feathers and favourite toys which can all be displayed at a level where the children can see and handle them. You could even display small items in small containers to encourage the children to try some sorting activities.

● Provide opportunities for the children to express what they see, remember and imagine. Remember that any work based on imagination and memory will need stimulation through stories, poems and discussion, but allow the children the freedom to express their own ideas in their own way.

Autumn

Children's best efforts wil be based on real-life experiences.

Tools and materials

● Very young children need good quality paint and brushes and soft grade drawing pencils (2B or 3B), with which they will be able to make a wide range of marks. Chunky beginner pencils are also useful. Always aim to present any materials in an attractive and accessible way.

● Offer paint in a range of colours suitable for the task. If you want to avoid using water, provide ready-mixed paint of a custardy consistency with a brush for each colour. Some children in the reception class will, of course, have previous experience of paint and will enjoy the opportunity to use water-colour boxes and fine brushes as well.

● You can also provide wax crayons, chalks and felt-tipped pens. Challenge children to use these materials in a variety of ways, as experimentation and experience are a basis for all learning. Make sure that opportunities are included for three-dimensional work involving Plasticine, play dough and clay as well.

● Before starting work with the children always try out tools and techniques yourself. This is sometimes a salutary experience and is a reminder that it is impossible to work with inadequate tools and materials. It also enables you to identify pitfalls and potential problems in advance.

● When the children are working, emphasise the need to care for materials, for example, sharpening pencils when necessary and not snapping brittle chalks. If the children are using soft brushes, establish good practice from the beginning, making sure that the brushes are not left standing in water pots, that they are washed thoroughly after use and stored with the bristles uppermost.

Images and artefacts

● Think of interesting starting points from first-hand experience. For example, take in some unusual fruit and vegetables and talk with the children about the shapes, colours and textures they can see. Provide coloured chalks for the children to work with and give them opportunities to experiment with the chalks to find out how they mix and blend. Let them work on coloured sugar paper either in a similar or contrasting colour to the fruit or vegetables that they are drawing.

● Another starting point could be to take in a puppet and make it come to life for the children. Let them draw or paint pictures of the puppet, having an adventure.

Themes

Young children need to work from memory and imagination on themes which are familiar to them, for which they have relevant contributions to make. Focus on everyday events such as 'Myself', 'My family', 'Someone I am fond of', animals, vehicles, homes and houses, which are all appropriate starting points. The symbolism which young children use to represent their ideas can often communicate and express complex thoughts, and many of their ideas are generated from real-life feelings and happenings as well as familiar stories.

Introducing new key areas

Everything you have in the classroom, every story, poem, song, can be used to extend children's sensory experience. Materials-based exploration and play will provide the best stimulus and it's important to give children the opportunity to experiment with any materials before starting work. Always consider new ways of working as well, and introduce these where possible.

Drawing

As a reception teacher you may be receiving children at a stage before they have learned to 'please the teacher' or to feel in any sense that they 'can't draw'. At this age they will draw whatever is in their imagination or in response to marks already made and they generally draw to please themselves. This period of development is brief and fragile and it should not be hurried. Children will begin to represent things more directly, in their own time.

Most young children love the feel of different materials, including pencils, pens, pastel, chalk, charcoal and brushes and will be happy to simply enjoy the medium.

Painting

Make sure rich thick pigment is available in the primary colours (red, yellow and blue), secondary colours (orange, purple and green) as well as black and white, from which initially you, and later the children, can mix other colours. Encourage the children to mix colours as soon as

they are able and provide mixing palettes or plates.

Once children have learned to mix their own colours and shades, provide powder paint or ready-mixed paint. Use colour-mixing games (with you joining in) to teach the techniques of using appropriate thicknesses, and strategies for mixing colour.

Colour games

● *Can you fill this piece of paper with lots of different colours?*

● *How many different colours can you make using red, yellow and white?*

● *How many different colours can you make using ...?*

● *Can you make a thick line/a wiggly line/a line using thick paint/ a line using thin paint across a sheet of paper?*

● Divide a strip of paper into equal parts in the shape of a snake. *Can you put a different colour into each space to make a stripy snake?*

● Provide a piece of paper in the shape of a butterfly, cover it with wallpaper paste, paint one side with patches of red, yellow and blue paint and fold it over. Discuss what happens to the colours.

Practical experience will always be more important than theory with young children. The aim is to provide thick, vibrant and 'self rewarding' colours; colours which are enjoyable for their own sake. Later in the year some children may enjoy the opportunity to use transparent water-colour paints and finer, softer brushes for a very different experience.

Printing

Children of reception age readily respond to shape and pattern. In conjunction with shape awareness and recognition, they can be involved in choosing and grouping, and making patterns of all kinds. An awareness of surface pattern also lends itself to printing activities.

Use thick paint, putting a little into a flat tray and placing a small piece of thin cleaning sponge on top. Show the children how to press the object to be printed on to the sponge, pointing out that it will coat the object with sufficient paint for one or two prints.

In addition:

▶ point out patterns on fabric, wallpaper, shells and anywhere else you can find them;

▶ bring in a number of items with a bumpy surface and encourage the children to feel the raised pattern;

▶ print with hands and feet;

▶ use found objects: small pieces of sponge, cotton reels, nuts and bolts or a potato masher;

▶ fruit and vegetables can be used whole and rolled across the paper or cut in half or in slices for printing.

Collage

Tactile experience is important at this stage of the children's development and collage is an ideal way for children to enjoy a range of materials including card, wood and fabric.

● Offer opportunities for children to explore, handle and manipulate a range of materials and a range of surface textures both natural and manufactured. Include a range of fabrics and paper, seeds and dried grasses which can provide opportunities for pictorial and pattern reliefs. Always use effective adhesives – PVA is a good general purpose glue.

● The children can also make rubbings from collaged surfaces using the side of a large wax crayon.

Modelling

Children need opportunities to develop their awareness of form and space, to stick and join materials, and to use a range of appropriate hand tools safely.

Experience in handling forms and exploring texture can lead naturally into children manipulating materials, modelling, assembling and constructing three-dimensional work. Given the opportunity to manipulate malleable materials such as clay, dough and Plasticine, children will often develop their own ideas for the subject matter of their models. Some children are able to work directly and naturally in three-dimensions and this provides the most useful practice.

Vocabulary

Introduce activities in an exciting way and, when appropriate, continue to interact with the children as they are working, stimulating response and

building up appropriate vocabulary. Name the tools and materials which are being used as the children work. Use verbs such as *make, collect, paint, pattern, draw, print, model, stick, press* and *squeeze*. Include sensory words, for example *look, listen, touch, taste* and words to describe feelings *nice, horrible, happy, sad* and so on.

Developing key areas

Mark-making
Approaches
- Use a range of tools including hands, feet, pencil, crayon and paint.
- Offer different combinations of mark-making tools.
- Make as many different marks as possible with each tool.
- Change the surface for the children to make marks on (include a range of different papers and materials such as clay or sand).

Observations and comments
- *How did you make that mark?*
- *Can you make another one like it?*
- *How many different ...?*
- *Can you make a short/long/big/small/wiggly/straight ... line ?*
- *Can you make two marks at the same time?*

Evidence of success
- Different marks made with the same tool.
- Original and imaginative marks.
- Wide variety of marks.
- Combinations of marks.
- Placement of the marks.
- Manual dexterity.
- Use of language relating to the task.

Building on experience of colour
Approaches
- Vary the colours offered.
- Offer a range of paint textures by adding water, glue, sand or sawdust.
- Give a choice of brushes.

Observations and comments
- *See what you can do with this...*
- *Look at ...*
- *Why did you choose that colour?*

Evidence of success
- Response to the different qualities of the paint.
- Willingness to experiment.
- The way in which colours were chosen and combined.
- Personal statements in paintings.
- Interest in the task, and a vigorous approach.

Observational work
Approaches
- Pass around a familiar or unusual object to observe, feel and smell.
- Invite a visitor in, for example a vet, to bring an animal in for the children to observe and stroke (perhaps a rabbit).
- Take the children on an observational walk or into the school grounds.
- Bring in a colourful bunch of flowers and display them against a suitable background.
- Take easels outside on a fine day.

Observations and comments
- *Can you see ...?*
- *Look at its lovely ...*
- *What does it smell like/feel like?*
- *What shape is the ...?*

Evidence of success
- Involvement and enjoyment.
- Evidence of careful observation (accept whatever kind of approach they make at this stage).
- Observation of lines, shapes and patterns.
- Awareness of the form.

Work from memory and imagination
Approaches
- A favourite part of a story.
- 'Someone you are fond of'.
- 'My house'/'My family'/'My friends'.
- A favourite or precious possession.
- 'A big storm'.
- 'When I feel angry/sad/happy ...'.
- Giants, dragons, monsters.

Observations and comments
- *Think of ... can you imagine ...?*
- *What would you feel if ...?*
- *What is your favourite ...?*
- *Can you tell me about ...?*
- *Tell me about your exciting picture.*

Art

Evidence of success
▶ Responses to mood and feeling.
▶ Elaborate or expressive marks: spiky, curved, swirling, heavy, delicate.
▶ Expressive use of colour.
▶ Shape and linear movement.
▶ Location and configuration of the marks and colours on the paper.
▶ Choice of materials and tools to express emotion and represent ideas about their world.

Shape and pattern
Approaches
▶ Patterns linked to favourite stories (designs for a bedcover for Goldilocks or one of the bears).
▶ Printing patterns with hands and feet.
▶ Patterns made by printing with found objects (the end of cut Plasticene, a potato masher).
▶ Printed patterns made by rolling fruit or vegetables.
▶ 'A beautiful hot pattern'.
▶ 'A beautiful cold pattern'.
▶ A collaged pattern.
▶ Patterns made outside by arranging pebbles or leaves.

Observations and comments
▶ *Look at the lovely pattern on ...*
▶ *Can you show me the pattern on ...?*
▶ *How many different patterns can you make with ...?*
▶ *Can you make that mark again ... and again...?*
▶ *Can you make that pattern right to the edge of the page?*

Evidence of success
▶ Recognition of what a pattern is.
▶ Use of repetition.
▶ Random or ordered patterning.
▶ Use of a range of colours.
▶ Placement of the repeated shapes and use of the paper surface.

Texture
Approaches
▶ Offer a selection of textured objects and materials (hidden in a bag) for the children to feel (include fur, wool, cotton wool, scourer).
▶ Collect textured natural forms, for example, bark, leaves, the contrasting textures of a conker in its shell, broad beans inside their furry pod, shells, feathers.

▶ Bring in textured fruit such as hairy kiwi fruit or a fresh pineapple.

Observations and comments
▶ *Is it smooth or rough?*
▶ *Is it soft or hard?*
▶ *Do they feel different or the same?*
▶ *Can you tell me what it feels like?*

Evidence of success
▶ Awareness that surfaces look different.
▶ Recognition that things feel different.
▶ Recognition of hard and soft, rough and smooth.
▶ Use of appropriate descriptive vocabulary.

Form
Approaches
▶ Offer a variety of malleable materials such as dough, Plasticine, clay.
▶ Experiment with pushing and pressing.

Observations and comments
▶ *What does it feel like ...? Warm, cold, hard, soft, smooth ...*
▶ *Can you squeeze ...?*
▶ *Can you roll ...?*
▶ *Can you make marks with ...?*
▶ *What shape have you made?*
▶ *What happens if you press this into the clay/ dough/Plasticine?*
▶ *Does the shape you have made remind you of anything?*
▶ *Has it become something?*

Evidence of success
▶ Enjoyment of the materials.
▶ Willingness to explore the materials.
▶ Manipulative skills.
▶ Awareness of solid shape.
▶ Recognition of related vocabulary.

Display
Display is an important aspect of artwork and can be taken to include the whole classroom environment.

Consider making a 'class art gallery' to display the children's work in an exciting way. Any displays should be interactive where possible, with clearly labelled objects for the children to handle and sort. Include any related material which will help to provide a context for the display. Make

sure the children are aware that you are celebrating all the children's work and that all their responses are valued by you, and the other children.

Reinforce your approval of the children's work by asking them to hold their pictures up for the rest of the class to see or show them in assembly or sharing times.

Ideas bank

Sketchbooks
▶ All about me.
▶ My book of patterns.
▶ My experimenting book.
▶ My careful-looking book.

Wall display

Try the 'unit' approach with each child making or painting an object or image to provide a unit which will become an element of a large wall display or series of mobiles. Use themes such as shapes, patterns, faces, birds or fish. For an effective display, restrict the colour – for example, red, green, white and black. Encourage the children to devise their own units, don't be tempted to use a template which is a poor substitute for lively originality and gives a very flat final result.

Greeting cards

Making cards for Christmas and Mother's Day, when you feel you have to impress parents, you may be tempted to make the task so directed that it is scarcely the child's work at all. However it is possible to produce a presentable end product using artwork which is the children's own work.

Establish some restrictions such as:
▶ provide folded pieces of card;
▶ decide what size the children's work will be;
▶ let children choose from pieces of their work on patterns, people, faces, animals, birds, flowers;
▶ select appropriate tools and materials;
▶ sometimes restrict colours to be used;
▶ let children choose to use collage, painting, drawing or printing.

● Observational drawings mounted behind a window cut in card and finished with a bow, make ideal Mother's Day cards.

● For Christmas cards tear off strips of coloured tissue (use red, green, yellow) and stick them with thin PVA glue in layers on squares cut from plastic bags. Add a small, real flower (or another shape) and then paste over the whole thing. When it is dry, it will peel off the plastic and can be stuck behind a window cut in folded blue or black sugar paper to make a card with a stained glass effect.

Assessment

Bear in mind that, at this stage, children see holistically. For this reason interpretations of what they see may be symbolic or moving towards the visually real. It is important to respond sensitively to the questions children ask, the things they say, what they do and whatever they volunteer.

However it is possible to evaluate some of the following aspects of children's art endeavours at this stage. Consider:

- How have they used what we have given them?
- What have they done and what they are trying to do?
- What evidence is there of independent thinking and personal ideas?
- Have they been willing to experiment?
- Have they learned a new word/skill/technique?
- Are they growing more confident in their efforts?
- Have the materials been used in an imaginative way?

Physical Education

Physical education will probably be the first timetabled lesson in which reception children are expected to respond as a whole class. It involves changing, moving to a larger space away from the security of the classroom and moving amongst all the other members of their class, often using apparatus or equipment. For some children, many aspects of this will be quite frightening or demanding, while for others it will be exciting and exhilarating. Your role is to enable them all to feel secure in the larger space, and to provide a safe and encouraging environment in which they can enjoy, explore and develop their movement experiences, and use their energies in purposeful and positive ways.

In many schools, PE is timetabled three times a week, with one of the sessions outdoors in the playground. For your reception class this will usually mean one session for gymnastic-type activities with large apparatus, one session for dance and one for games activities. Some schools are also able to offer swimming as an additional activity.

It is possible that sometimes you could use this timetabled time for PE more flexibly, choosing to continue an activity on subsequent days while interest is buoyant. You might also be able to arrange a flexi-playtime for the class – a separate or longer playtime to allow for wheeled toys, small games apparatus or even use of the nursery outdoor play area.

You can also incorporate movement into other activities (such as story time or music activities), to enhance and deepen the learning that is going on in all areas of the curriculum. If you have a particularly young class, you may prefer to develop ideas in movement as possibilities spontaneously arise, to address some of the physical and creative Desirable Outcomes. These might include pushing and pulling, digging, chalking on the ground, large-scale construction, role play and using musical instruments. This allows you a choice of alternative activities to extend and diversify the movement possibilities.

Ideally, your children need a wide variety of movement experiences on a regular basis. Short, frequent, daily sessions are most beneficial. All children deserve the opportunity to enjoy their growing movement confidence and competence and you will find many opportunities to develop other aspects of children's learning (language, mathematical concepts) through their physical activities.

Many aspects of learning to move are similar in each of the areas of activity, so some general expectations are included before focusing on more specific expectations.

What should they be able to do?

When the children in your reception class start school, there will be vast differences in experience, interest, physique, temperament, attitude and effort. Whatever the experiences they have had, they will need to learn to move in a large space with others, on equipment or with apparatus safely.

To begin with, some of the children may find it difficult to concentrate on how they are moving *and* listen to your instructions at the same time. With the excitement of the new surroundings and the bigger space, they need to hear what you are saying and have plenty of warning (for example *aaaaand...stop!*) so that they can manage their bodies to stop the actions in which they are involved. By the end of the year most children will be quicker and more successful in controlling their bodies to come to a halt when asked to do so.

Through games which involve stopping, starting and moving about the space, children will also become more aware of others and their surroundings. They will need lots of encouragement and practice to 'look for another space' and to use all the space that is available. To begin with, they may herd together for security, or may not be sure what is expected of them, but by the end of the year expect most children in your class to be moving more independently, increasingly showing their awareness of space and others.

All children will be able to walk, run and jump (apart from those with specific physical impairments – see note on p115) when they start school, and many will have a wider range of actions which they can perform successfully. By the end of the reception year, they should be able to name these movements and be more aware of their own actions (for example lift their knees a bit higher; keep their heads up). Observe how they perform these basic actions and gently encourage standing/walking tall, running on the toes and using the arms in opposition (right arm forward with left leg forward) as they walk or run.

Although the sequence of progression through the stages of motor development is the same for most children, they do not progress at the same rate or at an even rate and so there will be a wide range of differences in the ways they achieve various actions/movements.

Key area: Dance

The beginnings of dance start with action rhymes and games, which provide a secure and familiar framework in which children can be encouraged to isolate different parts of their bodies and move them in time with music or sounds. Some children will be able to do this confidently and quickly with increasing control and co-ordination, while others will need lots of encouragement throughout their time with you to join in the movements fully. Some will show an increasing ability to use their imagination, to listen and respond to the music or rhythm, to observe and copy actions of others or to contribute ideas of their own.

The children will show varying degrees of control in basic actions like stepping, creeping, hopping, turning and jumping and should be beginning to respond to variations in speed (slowly/quickly) and strength (lightly/strongly) as indicated by clear, simple accompaniment.

They may have some understanding of direction, size and level but this will need to be developed. Using contrasting actions is an excellent way to heighten the experiences for the children, for example: big steps and little steps; forwards and backwards; high and low. They will gradually become more aware of their own body actions and those of others and will begin to express their own ideas if given a clear framework.

Key area: Gymnastics

The children need plenty of time to practise in their own way their natural actions of running, jumping, sliding and moving on all fours. Although they will probably be able to jump in different ways, for safety you should teach them to land on two feet, giving at the hips, knees and ankles. By the end of the year they will be more aware of the need for squashy landings and be more able to manage their bodies safely. They may not be so proficient at moving from one foot to the same foot (hop), but should be encouraged to try and practise in non-threatening situations. Give frequent suggestions to change over legs.

By the end of the year, you will notice some improvement in skill and confidence with strength and balance developing. Some children may have difficulty in combining running and leaping until they have co-ordinated the extra little push that is required in one step of the run, but phrases of movements (for example hop, hop, hop, jump, jump, jump) will help them start to change from one activity to another.

Most children will be able to balance and hold still shapes on some of the larger parts of their bodies (back, sides, tummy), and on two feet and all fours. Gradually encourage them to balance on smaller parts of their bodies (one foot, bottom, shoulders). With practice, they will increasingly be able to clarify these shapes (feet together or apart) and to name them (stretched out, curled up).

Children will have had very different experiences of using climbing apparatus when they join your class. Some will be excited and agile on the apparatus, while others may be much

more tentative especially with lots of other children around. Some will not be very aware of others, while they are concentrating on what they are doing, and will need to be reminded to look before they move or jump. For safety, they need to be able to stop, come down from the apparatus carefully, and sit away from the apparatus when asked to do so. With opportunities and encouragement they will develop general body management and control and be able to try some of their actions on chosen parts of the apparatus. By the end of the year you will have introduced them to handling mats and benches safely.

Key area: Games

Young children need space to move freely and to try different actions (jog, stride, jump, gallop). They will gradually become more able to stop, start, change direction and move out of the way of others. They should be able to select from and use a limited range of equipment when asked to do so and follow brief, clear instructions. As soon as possible they should be encouraged to take responsibility for looking after equipment and returning it to the baskets or storage areas.

By the end of the year most of the children will be able to release and guide (roll, tap, throw, kick, push) a ball with increasing accuracy towards a still target (between skittles, into a hoop, to a partner, or between markings on the floor or wall). Encourage them to take time to aim and to keep their eyes on the target. Most children will be able to stop a ball when it is rolled, or tapped to them (slowly and often quickly), and many will be able to catch a large ball or beanbag by bringing it into their chests, relying less and less on the body and more on just their hands.

After opportunities to practise, most of the children should be able to bounce and catch a ball with two hands in several positions (sitting, kneeling, standing) and to count the number of times they can do so.

Many will play alongside and with other children, but soon they should be expected to share equipment and take turns, although they will need help to do so. With reminders, they should increasingly become aware of other children playing so they do not disrupt them when they are retrieving their own ball or equipment.

Practical ideas

Children with physical impairment need to be able to join in PE lessons. How you arrange this does, of course, depend on the degree of impairment but generally speaking you should aim to focus on what they *can* do – on ability not disability. Encourage independence as far as possible, but also make use of helpers or a 'buddy' system enabling them to work with another child. Make sure that you allow enough time for the child to tackle the task – which you can modify by adapting the response suggested, the apparatus or the rules.

 ## Making a start

Dance

Action rhymes and circle games

● Start with songs and rhymes with actions with which the majority of children are familiar, including finger rhymes – see *This Little Puffin* compiled by Elizabeth Matterson (Penguin). Find different ways to make the most of these actions, practising them separately from the rhymes at times, repeating the actions and encouraging the children's movements to become bigger and larger than life.

● Use the space in different ways (with children standing in a circle, in lines or choosing a free space). Gradually, ask the children to make choices such as to find a different place, to shake a different part of their bodies or to wiggle their fingers high or low.

● Sing songs like 'Here We Go Round the Mulberry Bush' with some energetic actions *This is the way we jump up and down* or *stamp our feet*, or ask children to think of different actions which can be included with a rhyme or song (for example *This is the way we go to school*).

● Exaggerate the actions from number or nursery rhymes ('Five, fat sausages', 'Incy wincy spider', 'Jack-in-the-box') and include songs with actions such as 'The grand old Duke of York' (children can march individually, in pairs or short lines) or songs to develop body awareness such

as 'Heads, shoulders, knees and toes' (vary the order or include different body parts).

● Sometimes, if there is space, dance-like actions or rhymes can be included as part of story time. For example, use a 'follow my leader' activity, or marching and jumping on the spot before settling the children down to listen.

Gymnastics

● Start by encouraging and helping children to become aware of the space and others, and more aware of their natural body actions (for example running, jumping, climbing and sliding), before introducing new ones. Use positive encouragement when they begin to be successful; *I liked the way you used your arms to help you jump/moved on your tummy/went under the plank on your back.* Help them to look for spaces and try different ways of moving on hands, feet and body parts.

Teach jumping and landing softly and safely on the floor before suggesting higher jumps or jumping off benches and planks.

Apparatus

● Once the children are responding well, introduce them gradually to the lower climbing apparatus (planks, benches, mats, trestle-tables, platforms). Ideally, to begin with, try and have the apparatus set out ready for them to use and let them choose where they feel confident to go.

● Teach them to use the apparatus carefully, emphasising the safety factors (looking where they are going, keeping in a space, not getting too close to others, and moving quietly), so that they can concentrate on what they are doing. Encourage them to try different pieces of apparatus, perhaps half the class using half the apparatus and then swapping over.

● Establish a consistent routine for stopping, coming down and sitting down away from the apparatus; teach them not to sit on the mats which may still be in use by other children coming down from the apparatus. They will need constant encouragement to use the space well, particularly when there are favourite pieces of apparatus.

● Use a theme such as finding spaces (travelling and looking) to help the children focus on moving into empty spaces and away from others (on the floor and where there is a space on the apparatus).

● Encourage them to use their hands and feet, and other body parts as they move. For example, using their hands to pull themselves along the bench and using hands and feet to move across the mat.

Games
Class games

● Introduce and use class games to start or finish the lesson. First try those with which some children are familiar, like 'Statues' or 'What's the time Mr Wolf?', and gradually introduce new ones like 'Traffic lights' (stop still on 'red', jog on the spot on 'amber' and jog round the hall on 'green'; actions can be varied to include jumping or hopping), or the 'Numbers game' (children move freely around the space; instead of 'stop' say a number (for example 3) and children must get into groups of three).

These games will encourage listening, quick responses to your stop and start commands and will give the children the opportunity to become more aware of the space and others as they move. Avoid elimination in games, instead use children

who would have been 'out' or last to choose the next shape, number or action and then involve them in the game again.

Use a variety of actions (for example walk, jog, run, hop, jump, gallop, skip or stride) in these enjoyable, non-threatening situations and the children will have the opportunity to become more competent in their actions (for example 'Try this, try that', 'Simon says').

Equipment

Provide time for the children to be introduced to, and use, selected pieces of equipment individually, so that they all use beanbags, or half the class use small balls and half use large balls. Suggest they try some of the activities, help them to do so successfully, then give them time to choose and practise.

Beanbags

Working individually with a beanbag each, the children can try:

▷ different ways of passing the beanbag from hand to hand (in front of them, behind them, above their heads) and around parts of the body;
▷ stepping or jumping over and around the beanbag;
▷ picking the beanbag up and putting it down in different ways, perhaps with different parts of the body (for example two elbows, two feet);
▷ balancing the beanbag on different parts of the body.

Provide some opportunities for free choice in each lesson to allow the children to play individually, to choose and experiment with pieces of equipment and work at their own level. Several limitations may be needed, for example *choose a beanbag or a ball, keep inside the grid, keep it on the floor, keep it close to you.*

Developing key areas

Dance

Musical games

Play musical games like 'Statues' (freely or specifying shape: large or small; twisted or wide) or 'Musical hoops' – avoiding elimination (this requires lots of hoops/rope shapes on the floor). The class march or gallop to familiar music or a tambourine until the sound stops, when they jump into a hoop as soon as possible. As hoops are taken away by you, the children help each other to share until they are all huddled in a few hoops. The hoops can gradually be put out until they again have a hoop each. Alternatively you can say *Only use a red hoop...*

Actions

● Percussion can provide a simple stimulus for actions. For example, use a cymbal to encourage slow, continuous movements which gradually come to a halt, or tambour taps to encourage jerky, sudden actions of part or the whole body. Link silence with stillness and sounds to action as children learn to listen and respond.

● Try out, then repeat, travelling actions in short phrases with percussion or simple music accompaniment (for example walking, tip-toeing, creeping, marching, stamping, striding, skipping, slow stepping, floating, crawling, wriggling).

● Practise listening and stopping, and prepare the children with your words or accompaniment (for example gradually slowing down, or stopping suddenly like a statue). Involve the children in thinking of different ways of moving for example *Can you think of a different way to creep?*

● Introduce travelling in pairs or small groups as a 'follow my leader' activity or side by side.

● Use phrases of 16 or 8 beats to help your class use the space. Try variations (16 beats in one direction, 16 beats in another; 16 beats low, 16 beats high).

● Bring to life actions in stories. Fleeting reference may be made in story time to things like giant strides, crawling through the undergrowth or stirring the pot, and these can be practised to reinforce, enhance and develop the story action. Make these into phrases of action for example *big step and step and step and stop; step and step and step and stop.*

● Observe and develop a selection of the variations which you see (fingers outstretched, elbows high) helping the children to become aware of their own body actions and those of others. Encourage them to move in interesting ways and make unusual shapes or try new actions in response to the task set.

● Help them to feel the essential qualities of the movement (*lightly, quietly, slowly or quickly*) and to begin to understand words through their actions (*shiver, shake, shrink, flop...*).

Gymnastics

Introduce the children to handling mats and benches correctly. Divide them into groups of four and show them how to stand two at each side of the bench or mat, bending their knees, not their backs, to lift. Teach them to look in the direction of travel and keep together. Start with one group at a time, then two groups, then half the class when you feel they are managing safely and carefully.

Themes

● Introduce themes rather than specific skills as the main objective of the lesson(s). In this way they will be encouraged to think more about their movements and they will become more aware of the different ways they can use their bodies, for example making a wide shape on a different part of their bodies (backs, sides, tummies, on all fours or just feet). Encourage the children to select movements which are appropriate to the task set – this will give them a sense of achievement and purpose. Try out ideas on the floor, and then develop them on the apparatus.

● Encourage fuller and more varied use of the apparatus by using a theme like around, in and out, on and off. Focus on moving in and out of each other on the floor (vary pathways), moving in and out of the apparatus, and finding different places on the apparatus to get on and off.

Balance

● The beginnings of balance start with holding still shapes on large patches or parts of the body (backs, sides, tummies). Help children to clarify the shapes they are making and to become aware of the parts of the body they use to rest on. Encourage children to hold the shape still for the count of three before moving to a new space and trying another still shape. In this way they will be moving in their own time and in control of their actions.

❱ move in and out of each other and around the space (dodging and weaving).

Equipment

Help children to explore a variety of equipment, specifically challenging them to try a wider repertoire of actions (for example stopping, spinning, rolling, turning, balancing), and using balls and other equipment of different sizes, colour, weight, texture (airflow, tennis or sponge balls).

Travelling

● On the floor encourage different ways of travelling on the feet (hopping, jumping, walking, jogging) and begin to introduce different directions. Remind them to look behind them when moving backwards. Suggest they try different ways of moving on all fours (tummy up, back up) on the floor or climbing on the apparatus, and on tummies, backs, sides or bottoms.

● At times, during the floor work or the apparatus work, ask the children to choose their favourite ways of moving and to repeat them, trying ways to improve them.

Games
Footwork

Encourage children to:
❱ make patterns with their steps and jumps, sometimes using two feet, sometimes one foot;

Safety

Remind children, when they are using the equipment, to be aware of the space around them and others in it. Young children particularly will be concentrating on what they are doing rather than on the movement and vicinity of others around them.

Beanbags

❱ Carry and pass the beanbag from hand to hand as they move.
❱ Try to catch the beanbag in two cupped hands, start with little throws.
❱ Aim the beanbag, tossing or throwing it into a rope shape, hoop or box.

Ropes

❱ Jump over, in and out of rope shapes on the floor.
❱ Run in and out of the shapes on the floor without touching them, return to their own shape on the stop signal.

Large and small balls

▶ Carry the ball as they move, stop and start, and change direction.

▶ Roll and stop a ball in different ways (two hands, one hand, two feet, one foot ...).

▶ Give little challenges and suggest new ideas (for example: *try spinning the ball with your other hand; try balancing the ball on another part of your body as you walk*).

▶ Make a game of passing a small ball around the body, in different directions. Develop to passing around the ankles, from hand to hand over head, making a figure of eight around the knees.

▶ Make up a game of rolling and stopping with a partner. *Can you choose a different way to stand or sit?* (Back to back, looking through legs.)

▶ Tap the ball with hands or feet along the ground (emphasise very small taps, keeping the ball close to your hand or foot).

▶ Bounce and catch the ball with two hands. Try in different positions (sitting, kneeling, standing) or walking slowly.

Quoits

▶ Make patterns: jumping, hopping over and around the quoit.

▶ Twist, release and spin the quoit, then try to add another action before the quoit falls to the ground (for example jumping, running around it, clapping hands).

▶ Bowl and roll the quoit, walking alongside it and stopping it before it rolls into someone else.

▶ Carry the quoit, pick it up and put it down, jog around and return to the quoit.

▶ Balance the quoit on different parts of the body, while walking, jogging, hopping.

▶ Aim the quoit into a hoop or bucket. Make this more difficult by taking a step further away or standing on one leg.

▶ Pass the quoit around different parts of the body, (slowly then quickly).

▶ Pass the quoit to a partner over head, through legs, around the waist, under one leg.

Hoops

▶ Specify or ask children to make up patterns of jumping, stepping, and/or hopping in and out and around the hoop, and moving in different directions (sideways, forwards and backwards).

▶ Walk, bowl and stop the hoop; hula-hoop it around the waist, or skip with it.

▶ Spin and stop the hoop.

▶ Make up a game using the hoop individually or with partner.

Give time for free play when children can choose, practise and consolidate actions.

Made up games

▶ Provide opportunities for made-up games individually or in pairs using specified or chosen pieces of equipment. For example, make a pattern of bounces with your ball (with two hands, drop and catch here and there; drop and catch from knee/waist height) or beat your record, or specified action (for example rolling, stopping or bouncing). *Can you roll the ball through your partner's legs and stop it the other side three times, then change over?* (Watch fair shares!)

Individual challenges

Introduce challenges within a chosen or specified activity.

▶ Count: *How many?* (ways of picking up a ball or beanbag; bounces; times ball hits the target; times ball/beanbag is passed to partner without dropping).

▶ Beat your own record, practising to try to improve the number of times.

▶ Develop shared, co-operative challenges (for example *With a partner, how many times can you ...?*).

▶ Make the activity more difficult: moving in another direction (look where you are going!), use the other hand or foot, a bit further away from your partner/target .

▶ Try aiming games: knocking down skittles, rolling ball between cones, hoopla.

▶ Make your own target out of a cardboard box ('Aunt Sally').

These challenges introduce simple competitive games. Each child will be encouraged to try harder and make the action more difficult without the disappointment of not coming first, or not getting the highest number.

Ideas bank

Dance

● Helpful books: *Dancing Rhymes* Dorothy Taylor (Ladybird) (out of print – see libraries); *Action Rhymes and Games* Max de Boo *Bright Ideas for Early Years* (Scholastic).

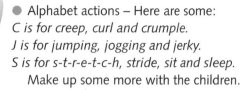

● Alphabet actions – Here are some:
C is for creep, curl and crumple.
J is for jumping, jogging and jerky.
S is for s-t-r-e-t-c-h, stride, sit and sleep.
    Make up some more with the children.

● Use characters or ideas from your topic or stories (for example for a Toy shop: jerky puppet, floppy rag doll, mechanical toy (strong and stiff), bouncy ball; 'Jack and the Beanstalk': climbing actions, giant strides).

● Objects can provide a focus of attention and give both a rich source of language and stimulation for movement. For example: bubbles – light, round, floating, turning, drifting and bursting; Jack-in-the-box – squashed and small, sudden change to stretched and open, slowly and quickly moving up and down.
    With encouragement and practice, the children will refine their actions through the use of words, and the way they are said (*st - r - e - t - ch* or *freeze!*), enhancing both their language and dance experiences.

● Praise interesting ideas and ask children to move again making part of the action clearer (*I liked the way you used your hands as well as your feet while you crept*). Encourage them to exaggerate the actions and to use their whole body in the movement, as some may be moving just part of their arms or legs.

● Use contrasting percussion to make a game out of listening and responding in movement; avoid eliminating children from the game. Experiment with a triangle or bells for light, gentle movements, sometimes quick, sometimes slow and use castanets for fast, jerky actions.

Gymnastics

● Large and small actions and shapes (size in stillness and action). Focus on making big steps/little steps, wide shapes/small shapes and so on. Use hands and feet and other body parts.

● Travelling and balancing – start to consolidate some of the actions introduced earlier, by suggesting children practise and then link different types of actions in one lesson. For example: travel using feet and then hold a still shape on hands and feet; travel on hands and feet and then hold a still shape on tummies, backs or sides.

Games

● Use balloons or light beach balls which are much lighter and slower than ordinary balls. Children will enjoy keeping them up in the air for several taps and catching them in different positions (above their heads, in front of them).

● Play some class games without apparatus, such as 'Action game' (for example seven pigeon steps, four giant strides...), 'Grandmother's footsteps', 'Oranges and lemons'.

● With apparatus – 'Back to my hoop' (move around hall not touching hoops, on signal, return to own hoop); 'Empty the basket' (you try to empty the basket of beanbags or small balls, distributing them over the space, while children return them, trying to prevent the basket being emptied); 'In and out of the beanbags' (children move about the space – walking, jogging, hopping – weaving in and out of each other and not touching the beanbags which are spread around the space).

Assessment

Because of the fleeting nature of physical actions, it is difficult to make detailed observations of a class of children constantly on the move. However, it is a good idea for you to get a general impression or overall feel for the class response.

Consider questions such as:

- How do the children respond, listen to my instructions/suggestions?
- How well do they:
  - think for themselves?
  - follow others?
  - do a bit of both?
- How well do they use the space? (Then think how they could be encouraged to use it better.)
- Are they able to use different directions? Are they aware of others when they do so? What could I say that might help them?
- How well do they sustain energetic activity?
- Are there other observations I need to make?

Review the class, focusing on a few children at a time. Try to watch how individual children respond and move. There will be times when you note achievement which is particularly significant and times when you look for specific actions or responses.

- Do they use the whole of the body when required?
- Which parts could they make more use of?
- How controlled are their movements?
- In which ways could they refine their movements?
- Can they talk about their own movements or those of others?

At this age children are often inconsistent in their actions, so be aware that there could be times when they may substitute one travelling action for another (for example a step down instead of a jump, a bounce jump instead of a hop).

Dance

- How well do they respond to my voice, the rhythm, sounds or music?
- How imaginative/creative are they?
- Are they achieving the qualities required?
- When? If not, why not? What might help?
- How well do they use individual body parts?
- Do they use some parts better than others?
- Do they use different levels of their own volition?

Gymnastics

- How do they use the apparatus? (Tentatively, boldly?)
- How inventive are their actions?
- Can they hold still shapes on large parts of their bodies?
- Can they take their weight confidently on their hands as they crawl or walk on all fours?
- Can they choose and repeat their favourite movements, or select appropriate actions?

(For example an action using hands and feet, a curled shape.)

Games

- How confidently do they move about the larger space?
- How do they stop, start and change direction?
- How confidently do they handle the different pieces of apparatus?
- How accurately can they roll or throw towards a stationary target?

At all times, take care to stress the positive aspects of the children's movement and enjoy and encourage their attempts. There will be as many different responses as there are children, and there will be many inconsistencies in response. Often excitement, stress or the many demands of a situation, particularly in games will cause the child to use less advanced movements.

Physical education

Information and Communication Technology

Children's aptitudes with computers may vary considerably at the beginning of this year, depending on access to computers either at home or in nursery or pre-school groups. Much of the ICT work introduced in school with reception children will be to get them used to using the computer effectively. This involves introducing the children to the three main input devices: keyboard, overlay keyboard and mouse, in a carefully-structured way.

Although the keyboard is generally the most common way of putting information into a computer, some reception children may have problems with pressing the keys effectively and with recognising upper case letters. However, some suppliers (for example RM) now provide replacement keyboards with lower case letters which may be more appropriate.

An overlay keyboard, (such as the concept keyboard) allows you to customise the input device so that sections of the keyboard can be designated as whole words, or even as a drawing. When the appropriate key is pressed the whole word will appear on the screen.

To use the mouse effectively requires considerable skill and practice. In many programs it is possible to slow down the movement of the mouse.

What should they be able to do?

Key area: Exchanging and sharing information

At reception level children need to be introduced to the ways in which information can be put into a computer. You can do this by talking to them about the wide range of uses which ICT has in the outside world, such as in supermarkets and banks, as well as making use of their own experiences of computers at home. Indeed, much of their initial work at school will be developing computer skills through games and other interactive activities.

During this year, children should be taught how to put information into a computer using an ordinary keyboard, an overlay keyboard and a mouse. Most children should be able to put their name into a basic word-processor and subsequently write simple sentences, using a word bank and concept keyboard. They should also have experienced the use of a database for inputting information and presenting it in a graphical way. Finally, they should be familiar with a simple floor robot and be aware that it can be controlled remotely.

You may have children in your class who have acquired considerable computer skills at home, and you will need to offer them more demanding activities. Use and develop their skills and confidence by enlisting their help to teach others, explaining that they must be patient and help the other children to do it themselves rather than simply doing it for them.

Practical ideas

🔵 Making a start

Talking-story CD-ROMs

A useful resource for young children comes in the form of talking-story CD-ROMs of which there is now a wide range available, many of which originate in the UK and so have English voices and spellings. Usually each page consists of a brightly coloured picture with some animation of the characters in the story. A few sentences of text appear and each word is highlighted as the words are spoken. Many contain a feature where clicking the mouse on particular parts of the picture makes further animation and sound occur.

Sit with a small group of children and listen to them repeat each sentence after it is spoken by the computer. Encourage the children to click on to particular graphic images to demonstrate the animations and sounds that can be activated. Using these CD-ROMs is an ideal introduction to using the computer and control of the mouse is developed as the children enjoy the story.

Visit a supermarket

Use a visit to a local supermarket (as part of a shopping topic) as an opportunity to look at bar-codes on each product. Try to arrange beforehand to use a till so you can show the children how a bar-code works.

Demonstrate that the bar-code can 'tell' the computer what the product is, how much it costs and then prints this information on a till receipt. If it isn't possible to arrange this, let the children watch the check-out procedure and then examine a till receipt.

Some supermarkets let customers scan in their own shopping, and with these systems it is easier to arrange for children to get first-hand experience. Here, you are emphasising to the children that ICT is used extensively in the outside world, and that computers come in different shapes and sizes.

Encourage parents to use their own shopping trips as opportunities to demonstrate to their children the use of bar-codes and computers, whenever possible.

Sliding puzzles

These programs consist of a full screen picture which can be broken up into a series of squares and then mixed up. Using a mouse or arrow keys, the children need to slide the parts of the picture around the screen until it is complete once again. This is useful as a problem-solving activity, with mouse and arrow key control being the ICT focus.

Variations on this activity allow for increasing the number of squares into which the picture is broken up, and using children's original artwork rather than pictures supplied with the program.

Adventure games

There are many 'adventure game' type programs that introduce concepts such as colour, shape and size through a number of screen-based activities which are set in interesting contexts. *Poldy the Scarecrow* (from Anglia), for example, has six activities where children can differentiate between different colours, shapes and sizes. In terms of their ICT capability, children will mainly develop mouse skills with this kind of activity.

Making simple pictograms

The software *Counting Pictures* (from Black Cat) can be used to introduce children to the way in which bar charts and pictograms actually work. Working as a group, get the children to look at a screen which contains a series of pictures at the bottom of it. Select the pictures from a library which comes with the program, to suit a particular topic on which the children are working. You may choose, for example, different pets that the children might have at home. Ask each child to say which is their favourite pet and to use the mouse to click on the correct image from the selection on the screen. As the children click on their chosen images in turn, a pictogram is

gradually built up, allowing the children to see how a graphical image can be used to represent numbers. It is then possible to replace the pictogram with a bar chart made up of different-coloured cubes. This helps children to realise the connection between numbers and the length of lines in bar charts.

Letter recognition

There are many programs available which concentrate on teaching children the shapes and sounds of individual letters. These use a combination of animation and sound (such as *Talking Animated Alphabet*). Initially introduce these programs in front of the whole class, using a large television screen which is attached to the computer. Afterwards individual children can work on screen to practise their skills. It is useful to have a range of software so that the important aspect of literacy work can be reinforced without becoming too repetitive.

On-screen wordbanks

Once children are able to use an ordinary computer keyboard, there will be occasions when they wish to communicate using a wider range of words. Software is available (such as *Clicker Plus* from Crick Software) which provides a customized on-screen wordbank which is displayed on part of the screen. When the children are writing stories using a word processor, they can type in some of the easier words, letter by letter, from the keyboard, then click on the on-screen word bank to select longer words to insert in their text. You will need to choose the words available to the children, to suit particular pieces of work. You may even wish to create a personalized wordbank for each child in the class. This could include their own names, their brothers and sisters names and perhaps where they live.

Introducing new key areas

Writing about myself

Let the children work on a concept keyboard whose layout includes all the words which are necessary for children to describe themselves in some simple sentences. Make sure it includes words such as : *I, am, four, five, years, old, have, green, blue, brown, eyes, fair, red , brown, black, hair and so on.*

When the concept keyboard is integrated with a word-processing program, the complete words appear on the screen as the appropriate section of the concept keyboard is pressed. At this point introduce the *delete* key as a way of removing mistakes. Also, show the children that the *shift* key can be used to change lower case letters into upper case.

Start the activity as a group discussion, finding out the words that the children want to use, and then produce the overlay to match the wordbank the children have devised. Suppliers of concept keyboards also sell programs which enable you to produce your own customised overlays, and ready-made overlays for particular activities.

Word-processors used on computers which have a sound card and loudspeakers fitted, are now able to 'speak' words as they are typed in. These programs (for example *Talking Word for Windows*) are extremely motivating for young children who are just beginning to use computers independently.

Making a graph

Introduce children to simple database facilities by asking them to select favourite items and enter the information into a database program. For example, ask the children to each choose their favourite coloured pencil. Ask each child to show you the colour he/she has chosen and get the children to input the data into a simple database program which can show information in a graphical form. Initially this will need one-to-one adult supervision.

Once all the information has been input, show the children what the resulting bar chart looks like on the screen. Discuss which is the most popular colour (the bar which is the tallest) and which is the least popular (the shortest bar). Finish off the activity by getting the children to bring their chosen pencils to you. Arrange them in rows. Discuss how the tallest row is the same

as the tallest line on the graph. This activity is a useful introduction to the way in which data can be easily analysed by using database programs.

Moving a floor robot

A variety of robots are available which consist of a vehicle which can be programmed to go forwards, backwards and turn round. At this stage the actual distances the robot travels are not really important and descriptions such as 'a little' or 'a lot' are all that are required.

Work with robots can be done as a whole class or large group activity. Starting with a robot in a fixed position in the classroom, enter in a command, such as *Forward 10*, and let the children watch how far the robot goes. Return the robot to the starting position and put in a command *Forward 5*; ask the children to predict how far it will go this time.

Now let children put in the commands, and ask them to stand in front of the robot just where they think it will stop. Develop this activity further with moving backwards, and then left and right.

At this stage, the children only need to be aware that it is possible to give instructions to a robot that it will follow, and that the larger the numbers the more it moves or turns. Combine this activity with work on learning 'left' from 'right'.

Developing key areas

Drawing a picture of myself

Ask the children to bring in a photograph of themselves from home. (Be aware of cultural or religious limitations on this among your children.) If some children do not have photographs

available, be prepared to take some shots in school. As a group, discuss the general features of photographs including the sizes, number and colour of features on faces.

Once the children have a basic understanding of facial features, introduce them to a paint package. Show them how to use the mouse to draw straight and curved lines and how to select colours and perhaps the size of the brush itself. Then ask them to draw a picture of themselves using the package and a mirror. Encourage them to focus on a few features of their face, particularly eye and hair colour. Depending on the availability of ICT resources at your school, this can be done over a short or much longer period of time.

Turn the pictures that they produce into a game, matching the photograph with the computer drawing, or use them as a display with the picture and photograph mounted side by side. This activity further develops mouse control both in terms of movement and in clicking the mouse button.

Teach the children how to use the *Print* command in order to print their pictures onto paper. Obviously, a colour printer is highly desirable.

Using an overlay keyboard

As children become more adept at computer use, they can be introduced to normal keyboards. Try using a card overlay to the keyboard to help familiarise them with the layout. Prepare a copy of a keyboard on cardboard for each child and ask them to colour in each function key as you introduce it.

The keys which are particularly important at this level are *delete* and *shift*. Get the children to add the lower-case letters to the keys for the

appropriate capital letters on their chart. This helps reinforce learning of capital/lower case letters and provides a reference tool.

Ideas bank

Dressing Teddy

Try using framework programs with the children, such as *My World* (from SEMERC) which allow them to fix already prepared images on to an existing background (like an electronic version of 'fuzzy felt'). These programs can be used right through the age range, with individual packages designed for specific age groups. *Teddy* (from SEMERC) provides the children with an unclothed Teddy and a wide range of clothes in which to dress him for a hot summer's day, and then for a snowy winter's day. Ask the children to produce print-outs of each picture to display on the wall. For a long-term project, get pairs of children to dress Teddy in an appropriate way for each day's weather. Display the pictures to provide a record of weather over a period of a month.

Making a card

Once children have had experience of using a paint package in a more structured way, they can draw a picture as the illustration for a birthday, Christmas or other greeting card, which they can take home. At this level, it is probably appropriate to just cut the picture out and stick it on the front of a folded sheet of A4 card.

Remind them of the features of any programs with which they are familiar, and introduce a few more facilities by demonstrating their use to individual groups of children. Some children, who are familiar with certain programs, will be able to take the activity further and develop their skills.

Assessment

By the end of the reception year you would expect children to:
● have used ICT as part of their work in a number of curriculum areas;
● have used story book CD-ROMs and be able to use a mouse to interact with the programs;
● have produced word-processed text using an overlay keyboard;
● be able to correct mistakes by using the *delete* key;
● be able to print work out using the *print* command;
● have produced some artwork using an art package, using the mouse;
● have input data into a simple database;
● have controlled a simple floor robot, making it move forwards, backwards, left and right.

Design and Technology

In the reception class, the aim of design and technology teaching is to introduce children to making something for a practical purpose. They should all learn to use some basic tools, such as scissors, correctly and acquire some experience of the working properties of materials (various kinds of paper, card, fabrics, plastics, foodstuffs and wood).

In addition, children should practise describing what they make and outlining its purpose. They should also learn to listen, take advice and follow instructions. A focused practical task, which you design and control to develop particular skills and provide particular experiences, will figure prominently in this work. When possible, however, children may adapt or take their product a stage further according to their own ideas. Sometimes they should also design and make a solution to simple practical problems.

Many design and technology activities in the reception class serve to widen children's experience and knowledge. However, it is important that the activities are structured so that a range of materials and new practical skills are introduced, and forethought, care and independent and co-operative working are developed.

Progression in these areas will prepare for and develop design and technology capabilities. Most of the children can attempt the tasks suggested although the nature and quality of their solutions to a problem will vary. This is differentiation by outcome. You may tune a task to particular children's capabilities by the way you present it. *How can we make our model spider jump and give everyone a fright?* and *How can we use this thread to make our model spider jump?* Always intervene if you can see a child getting frustrated or heading for irredeemable failure.

What should they be able to do?

When children start in the reception class, their knowledge, skills and know-how are likely to be very varied. Some will have 'helped' adults make things and some may have made

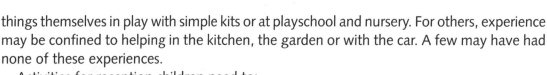

things themselves in play with simple kits or at playschool and nursery. For others, experience may be confined to helping in the kitchen, the garden or with the car. A few may have had none of these experiences.

Activities for reception children need to:
- develop their awareness of the manufactured world;
- introduce them to what counts in design and technology;
- provide opportunities to explore and widen familiar contexts;
- introduce some simple designing skills;
- introduce some simple making skills;
- increase technological knowledge and understanding.

Key area: Contexts

Design and technology activities can be drawn from your broader topics. Contexts and activities usually relate to personal needs, the family, the home, the school and the immediate environment so that the children understand them and see their relevance.

Key area: Making skills

Help children to:
- learn which tools to use for working on some common materials, like paper, card, thin plastic sheet, food and textiles;
- use templates to replicate shapes;
- follow instructions;
- practise marking out what they need;
- make practical suggestions about what to do next;
- learn how to join and combine some common materials and components and apply some finishes (such as paint).

Key area: Designing skills

Provide practical problems which give children opportunities to suggest ideas for solving them. Be ready to hint at possible solutions and to provide potentially useful clues. Help them express and clarify their ideas and watch for children who incorporate effects which are to be imagined. For instance, faced with the problem of making a door which opens in a cardboard box, a child may draw one on the box and pretend it opens; this is what they are used to in their play. You may have to remind them that what you want it to do is to open like a real door.

Encourage children to practise a variety of ways of communicating their ideas. Initially, they may draw their product or solution after they have made it. Eventually, they should begin to draw it first.

Key area: Knowledge and understanding
Materials and components

Children's experiences of materials like paper and wood may be limited to a narrow range of types and forms. They will need time to explore a material's types and forms and to learn of its capabilities. For instance they may not have felt the increase in strength which results

Design and technology

from folding paper or its springiness when pleated or lightly crushed.

Use activities to explore properties of this kind, and the development of vocabulary to accompany them, before introducing making and problem-solving with the materials. Focus on one new material at a time and then provide further activities to consolidate experiences.

Reclaimed materials (boxes and tubes) are useful and the children can be encouraged to bring these from home. Large, child-sized products may be easier for them to manipulate. However, activities should also include work with paper, card, felt, thin sheet plastics, kits, foodstuffs, and some experience of the properties of wood.

Mechanisms and control

Reception children can become aware of and make simple mechanisms such as hinges. You could start by showing them real hinges on doors, boxes, desks, spectacles and spectacle cases and then get them to make a hinge with adhesive tape and a card flap. This could then be used as part of the task of making a model house, from a card box.

Structures

Explore together the way in which materials can be given enhanced properties by folding, shaping or combining. For instance, paper can be folded to make hats and books, and boxes or kits can be used to build walls, which can be compared with the real thing.

Products and applications

Children should investigate how toys, classroom objects and safe household items have been made, assembled and finished to make them suitable for their purpose. Children can compare different versions of the same thing, for example, spades in the sand tray. *Which do you like best? Why?*

Quality

Encourage children to take care over what they make and the quality of the result, finishing their work as neatly as they can.

Health and safety

You cannot assume that young children are aware of the need for safe practice. Ensure that the materials and tools they are using are safe and that you can always see the work area. Explain simple safety precautions, demonstrate how to use and carry tools and equipment safely.

Materials often come in large pieces; cut them to a manageable size (this also prevents some wastage). Children's scissors are, by necessity, small and blunt-ended and this can make fabric cutting difficult, so avoid providing pieces which need extensive shaping.

Vocabulary

Extend the appropriate vocabulary for what they are using and doing. Introduce the correct words and reinforce them whenever possible (for example 'hinge', 'bricks', 'mortar').

Working levels

Accommodate work at various levels by altering the degree of support you provide to individual children. An alternative is to use a context which allows a variety of possible products (for example different hat styles). You might then allocate tasks or otherwise ensure that children are working at an appropriate level.

Design and technology

Design and technology

Practical ideas

Making a start

If you are working on a specific topic, this could provide a good starting point for design and technology activities.

Contexts

Stories

Many stories, rhymes and songs with which the children are familiar can provide a basis for design and technology activities. For example 'The old woman who lived in a shoe' could introduce activities on building model houses.

Visits

Visits which relate to other areas of the curriculum can have a design and technology element. A visit to the sea-shore for instance, could lead to making boats.

Visitors

Visitors who can bring in things relating to what they do can be a source of simple problems to solve. The school crossing person for instance, might talk about road safety and his or her special coat. *How might you make yourself easily seen?* This could lead to the children making armbands from brightly coloured felt.

Support making

Support for making can depend on what you do before the lesson. Materials that are partly shaped and limited in range point the children in the right direction. During the activity demonstrate the appropriate skills to provide an example of good practice, talking about what you are doing as you demonstrate or guide them through a task. Have clear targets about quality in a particular task (for example symmetry, an even coat of paint, straight cuts), show concern for quality in what you do and praise it in the children's products.

Designing and problem-solving

Ensure that the children know what the task means and what it encompasses. Ask questions to stimulate the recall of relevant knowledge and

to practise new vocabulary. Supplement this knowledge. Ask for ideas and be prepared to provide hints and clues.

Develop new knowledge

Everyday objects can be used to develop new knowledge. The children can examine them and explain to you how they work. Give them things that can be safely dismantled and re-assembled (for example a play person figure).

Introducing new ideas

Contexts for designing and making

In each of these examples, an introduction is provided, a related practical task is described and further development is given. These ideas illustrate ways of introducing new activities and you can adapt them or use them as models for other activities.

Paper and card: badges

Point out to the children that they each have a peg in the cloakroom for their coats. *How will you remember which is yours? What could you make to help you remember?*

Prepare some animal shape templates in advance and show the children how to use them. Cut out a card shape and illustrate how it will make a distinctive marker for a peg. Discuss how it might be hung on a peg (for example a loop of string held in place with adhesive tape). The children can now make a shape for themselves and decorate it distinctively.

The children can now design and make badges to wear so that you will know their names. Make

one and wear it yourself to demonstrate the task and to show one way of fixing it to clothing. An extension is for the children to make a name plate for their bedroom door, punching holes in an animal or plant-shaped piece of stout card to take a loop of string to hang on a door handle. A variation is to use a rectangle of card to which the children glue a small picture of their choice.

Fabrics: bookmark

Point out to the children that they need something to show their place in their reading books. Folding the corner of a page spoils the book. *What can you use?*

Provide a range of bookmarks made from different materials for the children to examine, ending with those made from fabrics. Introduce felt and let the children handle it and sense its properties. Demonstrate how to cut out a bookmark shape and how to decorate it, and then let the children design and make one.

Show the children a tray which has been marked by a plate or cup and ask them if they can think how this could have been prevented. Direct their discussion towards making a felt placemat. The children can then design and decorate one to take home.

Reclaimed materials: houses and homes

Read *The House at Pooh Corner*, A A Milne (Mammoth) or a similar story. Discuss what a house is and what it consists of.

Show the children how to use a card box (a shoe box is ideal) to make a house. Discuss how they might make a hinged door and a window with 'glass' (transparent plastic). They can then make and decorate the exterior of their house for a particular person or animal to live in.

Discuss what furniture is needed for the house and how they could use reclaimed materials to

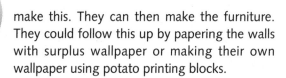

make this. They can then make the furniture. They could follow this up by papering the walls with surplus wallpaper or making their own wallpaper using potato printing blocks.

Wood: itches and tickles

In a topic such as 'Ourselves', talk about itches and tickles. *What parts of our bodies can't we reach? How can we scratch an itch on our backs?*

Discuss how ready-cut lengths of strip wood (for example 1cm square cross-section) could be used to solve the problem. *What could we put on the end to do the scratching? How could it be fixed to the wood so it does not fall off when it's used?*

What things tickle people? *Can you design and make a 'tickling stick' from a straw and fluffy fabrics or feathers?*

Food: fruity animals

Ask the children which fruits they like to eat. *What is your favourite fruit? What shape is it?*

Show some pictures of animals (for example hedgehog, snail, mouse) and bring out a range of fruits. Ask the children which fruit looks like a hedgehog. Use half a pear and decorate it to look like a hedgehog (using flaked almonds, currants, liquorice laces).

The children can then design and make their own fruit animals.

Using kits

There are several different kinds of kits available. Some make a limited number of items (such as a caterpillar or aeroplane) and these can be useful for practising dismantling and assembling. Other kits are systems which can be used to build a wide range of models (LEGO, Sticklebricks and so on) and these may be used to model houses and furniture, for example.

Children who are not familiar with a kit need some time to learn its properties. Show them how to join pieces and let them experiment for a while. Make this play purposeful as soon as they are familiar with the components. Begin with a specific task: *See if you can make a table.* Extend it. *What goes with a table? Can you make a chair?* Then set a simple problem. *Think about a room in your house. Which one are you thinking about? Can you make some of the things you have in that room?*

Ideas bank

● Use paper and card to make decorations, paper hats, place markers and doilies for a party. Extend the work by making Christmas tree and/or table decorations and printing wrapping paper for gifts and gift cards.

● Make a house for a purpose. The children could make houses for the Three Little Pigs from straw, twigs and bricks (use modelling clay) and test the structures to see which the wolf might be able to blow down. An extension would be to make a child-sized house using large boxes as building blocks.

● Use rectangular blocks of wood to print brick wall patterns with paint. These can be used to decorate the exterior walls of cardboard box houses.

● Make a bridge for the Three Billy Goats Gruff using construction kits.

● Let a draught of air blow papers from your desk. *What can I use to prevent that happening.* They can make paperweights from clay (the kind which does not need to be fired), shaping them

and decorating them to look like fruit or animals. Let them take them home as a gift.

● Using large cardboard boxes, the children can design and make furniture for the home corner. A washing machine, cooker and television can be made in this way. Furnish a book corner or a shop in a similar way.

● In a 'People who help us' topic, when discussing how we are helped when we are ill or injured, show a variety of items (for example sling, sticking plaster, bandage, crutch, walking stick, neck collar). Discuss what they might use for an eye injury. Use this to lead to designing and making an eye patch for teddy. Extend this work to caring for pets, for example making a card cone of the kind used to prevent a dog from chewing a bandaged leg.

● Seeing a stuffed toy made is a useful experience for young children. Choose a simple design, cut out the pieces or draw them on the cloth for children to cut out. You stitch them together, showing how a margin was left for this purpose. Turn it inside out to present the correct side of the cloth. Let the children stuff the toy.

Watching, discussing and contributing to the making helps to raise children's awareness of what is involved in making with fabrics.

● Make a variety of model furniture from small boxes, for instance, a bed from a shoe box with covers cut from fabric remnants or a table from an upturned box with a square of fabric as a tablecloth (cut away parts of the sides to leave legs at the corners). Cut plates from card and draw food items on them. Use bottle tops as cups or introduce clay to make thumb pots. The children could then be asked to design and make a chair to fit the table. These could accompany a reading of 'Goldilocks and the Three Bears'.

● Ask the children to design and make a costume for a fancy dress party. The outfit could be for a super hero, or for a fairy tale or pantomime character and should include the props to go with the costume (a fairy's wand, for example). Provide cartons, bin bags (cut open), lengths of wood, card, paint, pieces of fabric, colourful buttons, glitter, glue, pieces of ribbon, wool and elastic. A mixed project of this kind develops knowledge of, and practises skills in, working with a range of materials.

Assessment

In design and technology, you need to assess both the children's knowledge and skills. While a finished product can provide some evidence of skills, it cannot tell you everything you need to know. In particular, you need to know about those skills which are not evident from the product. For instance, did the children suggest ideas of their own? Did they suggest the next thing to do? Did they work tidily? To make an assessment of this you need to observe them as they work and keep brief notes.

What do they know?

This is not closely defined but they should know some simple properties of materials such as paper, card, thin plastics, fabrics, foodstuffs and wood. They should be able to describe these in terms such as 'hard', 'soft', 'bendy', 'stiff'.

They should know that many objects in their home and school environments are made or manufactured and they should be able to identify some.

They should know which cutting/shaping tools are appropriate for the materials in the tasks they have tried.

What can they do?

They should:
- begin to generate ideas when handling, shaping and rearranging materials and components;
- begin to describe what they want to do;
- be able to copy simple, demonstrated techniques to shape, assemble and join materials;
- be able to name what they are making and the materials they are using;
- be able to state how they will use their products;
- begin to provide a simple evaluation of their products in terms of personal satisfaction and give an indication of the reason for that;
- be able to describe how a simple object from a familiar context works, albeit imprecisely at this stage (for example a pencil sharpener, scissors, a hinged box lid, a safety pin).

Religious Education

Religious Education, unlike the subjects of the National Curriculum, has to be planned from a local rather than a national document. Agreed Syllabuses differ in the way they present the Programme of Study but are remarkably similar in what they expect children to do in RE. It is very likely that your Agreed Syllabus expects children to:

- develop a knowledge and understanding of religious traditions;
- explore fundamental questions arising out of people's experience of life;
- develop their own ideas and values arising partly out of what they learn in RE.

In terms of continuity and progression in RE you should be helping your children to develop a systematic knowledge and understanding of some religions, as well as developing their thinking about religious issues and understanding of common themes across religions, which will contribute to their understanding of religion in general. Some Agreed Syllabuses give guidance or a programme of study specifically for nursery and reception, however, in general, Agreed Syllabuses begin their Programme of Study at Key Stage 1. Therefore, in the majority of cases you can base your approach to RE in the reception class on the requirements for Key Stage 1, as well as referring to the early learning goals for personal, social and emotional development.

In the early years an emphasis is often placed on the human experience approach to RE. This focuses on an important question or issue about life, such as 'Who is my neighbour?' or 'Why are we here?' This question is then explored by looking at a number of religious responses to it. This approach lends itself to exploring religious education through integrated themes or topics. This is entirely appropriate as long as there is coherence across the curriculum.

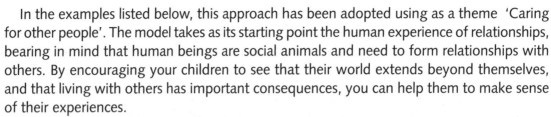

In the examples listed below, this approach has been adopted using as a theme 'Caring for other people'. The model takes as its starting point the human experience of relationships, bearing in mind that human beings are social animals and need to form relationships with others. By encouraging your children to see that their world extends beyond themselves, and that living with others has important consequences, you can help them to make sense of their experiences.

By introducing the children to some common values, found in a variety of religious traditions, their experiences of human relationships and their thinking about them can be broadened and deepened. The emphasis is on the belief that people should love one another – which is common to many traditions and is sometimes referred to as 'the golden rule'.

What should they be able to do?

Reception children come to school with a variety of experiences about religion and human relationships, some will have experience of formal religion, while others will not. You can hope that most of them will have some experience of, and be able to talk about, what it means to be loved and to love someone else. Such experiences form the basis of the theme used in this example.

Much of their learning in school will take place within the context of play, story and conversation. An important thing you can do in RE with reception children is to encourage them to develop their ability to use language appropriately to express emotions, opinions and values. You can also help them to raise questions about the kind of experiences which prompt religious and ethical responses to life, and extend their learning by introducing them to unfamiliar experiences. In doing so, you can help them to understand why other people believe and behave as they do.

Children at this early stage of schooling can also be encouraged to develop a confidence in their own sense of identity and to show a willingness to recognise the needs and feelings of others. As part of this topic you can also give them the opportunity to develop some important knowledge of stories, including stories from religious traditions, of loving behaviour and how religious communities express love through giving.

Key area: Knowledge and understanding of religions

Reception children develop their knowledge and understanding through direct contact with people, concrete situations and stories. In this topic, such knowledge is not approached in a systematic way but the theme of caring for others provides a structure for exploring some key ideas from religious traditions about human relationships. The major religious traditions share the belief that humans should love one another. For example, the Christian is asked to 'love your neighbour as yourself' (the second great commandment), the Muslim should 'show kindness to the neighbour who is related (to you) as well as the neighbour who is a stranger' (Qur'an Surah 4) and for the Sikh, 'there can be no worship without performing good deeds' (Guru Granth Sahib 4).

Concept development is an essential component of good RE teaching at any level. The range of religious concepts that can be explored in this topic include charity in Christianity, zakat (almsgiving) in Islam and sewa (service) in Sikhism.

To help children to gain some understanding of such concepts, you can use this topic to introduce them to stories from the religious traditions. You can also give them the opportunity to meet people of different faiths and to learn something about their lifestyle.

A very important aspect of good RE teaching is the raising of fundamental questions. In this topic, the knowledge that we hope children will gain about the religious traditions comes from asking 'How do religious people show love for others?'. Other important questions that can be explored in this topic are dealt with in the other two key areas.

Key area: Exploring human experience

An important part of children's early years school experience is to learn to respect and be polite to each other and show care and concern for others. RE is no different from the rest of the curriculum in this respect. However, RE can contribute to children's learning in this area by focusing on specific human concepts and by raising important questions about human experience. Encourage the children to talk about concepts such as love, fairness, goodness and giving.

From discussion of such ideas, you can then help them to reflect on and talk about such questions as: *How can we show someone that we love them? How do we know when someone loves us? When is it easy and difficult to show love? Should we only love those people who we know?* Such questions are not only important in themselves but they form a basis from which children can approach the stories and experiences indicated in the last Key area.

Key area: Responding to religion and human experience

Responding to questions plays an essential role in this area. Encourage the children to respond to the type of questions outlined in the first two Key areas. Show them how to answer such questions with statements like 'I think...' or 'I believe...'. This helps them to appreciate that people can respond to important questions in their own way, which will help them to develop positive attitudes such as respect for others' points of view. If there are children from a variety of faiths in the class, encourage them to talk about aspects of their families' lives and places of worship which illustrate forms of loving behaviour. This can help these children to form a positive self-image, while the rest of the children learn to recognise the needs and feelings of others. Such attitudes are not only important in themselves but are essential if children are to understand the concepts identified in the other Key areas.

Practical ideas

Religious education

Making a start

Use photographs

Ask the children to bring into school photographs of people who love them or of people who they love. Be prepared for anything! Children often like to bring in photographs of pets. Make sure you keep the topic focused on the way you want it to go. You can then encourage the children to share these pictures and to talk about them.

Arrange a discussion

Develop this by exploring with the children how people can show love. Examples may be giving presents, writing a letter, giving a picture, hugging or kissing and holding special celebrations like birthday parties. Make a list together of all the different ways that people show that they love someone.

Tell a story

Having focused the children's attention, you can then take the theme further with the help of a good story. The Good Samaritan is appropriate as long as you can get hold of a suitable version; try the *Young Puffin Book of Bible Stories* (Penguin). If you enjoy telling stories, make yourself very familiar with the Bible version and then retell it yourself. Whatever version you use, you will probably have to explain some of the language as there are words that may be unfamiliar to the children, for example *priest, temple, Samaritan* and, in this context, *neighbour*. You can put these on flash cards and talk about their meaning. Concentrate particularly on the word 'neighbour' since it is important to make it clear that this word can mean more than just the person who lives next door. Start with some key questions to set the context, for example: *When is it easy and difficult to show love? Should we only love those we know?*

Discuss the story

The point of the Samaritan story in this context is to extend the children's understanding of what it means to act in a loving way. Use questions to help you discover how well the children have understood the story and to give them a chance to offer some reflections. *Who was the neighbour to the man? Why do you think the other two men did not help him? Are there any times when you could have helped someone but didn't? Why did Jesus say, 'Be like the Samaritan?' What is the story telling us to be like? Should we help only those who are our friends?*

Other good stories from children's literature to extend these issues are:
Shan Helps Rani Mary Dickinson and Meena Jamil (out of print, try libraries), *Alfie Gets in First* Shirley Hughes (Red Fox).

Prepare a worksheet

Prepare a worksheet of pictures showing some people helping others (such as a nurse or a crossing patrol person) and others that don't show this. Ask the children to colour in or circle those pictures that show loving/ helping behaviour.

Introducing new key areas

Develop this initial work on loving and helping by exploring what it means to give and to share.

Bring in something precious

Ask the children to bring in something very precious to them which they would hate to lose (a favourite teddy for example). If necessary, label any duplicates with the owners' names. You could wrap the items up and see if the other children can guess what is in the packages, before opening them and talking, with the help of the owners, about why the objects are special and how it would feel to lose them.

Talk about a word

Talk about the word 'gift'. Relate the word to the children's idea of presents. *Which of the children's special things were gifts?*

Read a story

Use Shirley Hughes's story *Giving* (Walker Books) to explore with the children lots of different ways in which people give things. This will help to extend their understanding of giving in familiar settings, for example there is a reference in the story to somebody giving up a seat on the bus.

Sharing

Ask the children what they like to share with others. You can talk about such things as sharing sweets or toys with which all children will be familiar. Try and extend the discussion to more personal examples such as sharing our time with other people, perhaps in terms of playing with others or looking after someone who is new in the class. Refer back to the Shirley Hughes story *Giving*. In the reception class, this could be extended to the idea of spending time looking after each other as the children are all new. Focus on the question *What does it mean to share ourselves?*

Read the story of *John Brown, Rose and the Midnight Cat* Jenny Wagner (Picture Puffin) to the children. John Brown is a dog who lives happily with Rose, but when a black cat tries to join the family John Brown wants nothing to do with it. Eventually he realises that he has to share Rose's affections or risk destroying their relationship. Another good story to read aloud is Shirley Hughes's *Dogger* (Red Fox).

Draw a picture

Talk to the children about why John Brown didn't want to share himself and then why he had to. Talk, perhaps, about how brothers and sisters have to share their parents' attention. *Do you sometimes find it hard to do this?* Then ask the children to draw a picture of the story that illustrates its message.

Bake a cake

Bake a cake together and share it between the children, or with another class.

Make a collage

Make a class collage for display that illustrates all the things that we can share with other people. Children can draw pictures or cut them from magazines. Alternatively make a collage of the class – using self portraits or photographs – showing who shares what with whom, for example 'David shares his football with Aaron'.

Do some drama

Try some simple drama in which the children can show how we can share friendship and love. For example, saying things like 'thank you', welcoming people by shaking hands, hugging or helping each other.

Learn about a religion

Make use of a resource such as The Westhill Project *Life Themes in the Early Years* (Pack 3), Relationships and look at the picture of Muslims giving sadaqah (voluntary giving of money to support a mosque or people in need). Explore the kind of things people give money to and the reasons behind the giving. Link this to work on fundraising (see page 128).

Developing key areas

The three key areas of RE listed here, describe both the content of RE and the process of teaching it. Because the areas are inter-linked, they are not separated in this section but are referred to in the examples given.

How religious communities care

You can extend the children's understanding of caring for others by introducing them to how some religious communities show care.

Invite a visitor

Invite a Salvation Army Officer or a Christian Missionary into school to talk very briefly and simply about their work. Ask them to give examples of how their work illustrates the concept of Christian charity or love. Prepare some questions with the children in advance.

Take them on a visit

An ideal visit with children is to a Sikh Gurdwara. An essential part of Sikh spirituality is 'sewa' or service and you can experience this in the langar or free kitchen. As a visitor you will always be offered something to eat or drink as an expression of 'sewa'. Sikhs will also be happy to talk to you about other expressions of 'sewa' in which they are involved.

In preparation do a class letter, signed by all the children, asking if you may visit. As a follow up, make and send a class thank you card. Make a class book about the visit which could include photographs, drawings and writings.

For advice on visiting places of worship contact your local RE Centre.

Look at some posters

Use commercially produced photo packs (such as those produced by Westhill, Folens or Nelson) that show religious communities caring for others. Use the pictures for discussion and ask the children: *What can you see in the picture? What do you think the people are doing? How do you feel when you look at the picture? What does the picture make you think about?*

Fund-raising

Involve the children in a fund-raising project, this might be part of a larger school initiative or something with a personal or local link. Explore some of the ways that giving money can help other people in need. Choose a suitable organisation, such as the Children's Society, Christian Aid, Federation of Jewish Relief Organisations, Help the Aged, Islamic Relief, Oxfam, Save the Children Fund, Shelter, Sikh Cultural Society.

Responding to stories from the religions

Read together a number of stories from the religious traditions which will enable the children to reflect on ways of caring for others. Some of

the best examples are to be found in the Sikh and Muslim traditions. A short list is included below. You may need to consult your RE resource centre for some of these.

Sikhism

Suitable stories from the life of Guru Nanak are called the *Janam Sakhies*. They include a story about Nanak and the poor, sometimes called 'A Good Bargain', which children enjoy. If you can't find a copy of the *Janam Sakhies* try a publication called *Neighbours* published by RE Centre, Brunel University, Osterley Campus, Borough Road, Iselworth, Middlesex TW7 5DU, telephone 0208 891 8324.

There are a number of useful stories in *Stories from the Sikh World* published by Macdonald (out of print).

Islam

A good story is 'Caliph Umar Helps the Poor and Hungry' which can be found in a book called, *Stories of the Caliphs* (The Islamic Foundation). Another book from the same source is *Love Your Brother, Love Your Neighbour*.

Ideas bank

Caring for other people is only one possible topic within the theme of relationships. The ideas in this section are for some extension topics/ activities which explore more aspects of the human relationship theme introducing the concept of learning from others.

People who teach us

Talk about those people from whom we learn things: teachers, mums and dads, brothers, sisters, and so on. Explore some questions like: *What do we learn? Who teaches you? What are the most important things we can learn?'*

Get the children to draw pictures and make a display of all the people at home, in school and in the community from whom they learn.

Read a story

There is a large range you could use, including: *A Baby Sister for Francis* Russell Hoban (out of print), *Brothers and Sisters* Sue Perry and Norma Wildman (A & C Black), *The Boy Jesus in the Temple* Luke 2, v 41-52, 'Story of Guru Nanak' *Stories from World Religions* series (Heinemann).

Look at some pictures

Choose some pictures which illustrate children learning from other people. A good source is The Westhill Project *Life Themes in the Early Years* (Pack 3), consult your local Resource Centre.

Invite a visitor

Invite a visitor from a religious community such as the local vicar, rabbi or imam. Choose a person who understands small children and is used to talking to them. Ask your visitor to talk about what he/she does to teach children in the community. Afterwards encourage the children to draw a picture and write a few words about the visit.

Learning from books

As a follow up, look at the holy book connected with the visitor such as The Bible, The Torah or The Qur'an.

More stories

Some other stories to support your work on aspects of relationships are in the series *Talk about books*. Titles include 'My Mum', 'My Dad', 'Sisters and Brothers', (Annick Press). These are especially good for children to look at by themselves. Also see: *Grandfather and I* and *Grandmother and I* H Buckley and J Ormerod (Puffin Books) and *The Patchwork Quilt* Valerie Flournoy and Jenny Pinkney (Puffin).

A very good guide for stories in RE in general is *Tell Me a Story* by Maurice Lynch, available from the RE Centre, Brunel University, Osterley Campus, Borough Road, Isleworth, Middlesex TW7 5DU, telephone 0208 891 8324.

Assembly ideas

Many aspects of this work can contribute to ideas for class or group assemblies. A useful resource which includes some of these ideas in assembly form is *Action Plans: Assemblies* (Scholastic). Themes of 'Caring for others', 'Learning from others' and 'Making up with others' are included. These A4 cards contain the text of some of the stories included in this chapter along with poems, prayers and hymns.

The *Themes for Early Years* series (Scholastic), aimed at leaders and teachers working with children up to and including their reception year, also includes specfic assembly ideas.

Assessment

When you have finished this topic you will have a pretty good idea whether the children have enjoyed it. You should also be able to judge by the outcomes how much they have learned.

What do they know?

The emphasis in this topic is not, essentially, on knowledge of religions. However from their experiences gained during the topic most children should know:

- some stories, including those from religious traditions, of loving behaviour;
- some of the ways in which religious people care for others.

What can they do?

In a typical reception class you can expect children to respond at different levels. In this topic, for example, you can expect all or most to be able to:

- talk about their experiences of loving behaviour;
- retell the basic elements of a story;
- talk about their experience of a visit to a place of worship.

You can expect some children to:

- understand and explain why people behave towards each other in kind and unkind ways;
- explain something of the meaning of a story.

What have they experienced?

The children should have:

- listened to stories about loving behaviour;
- engaged in discussions;
- visited a place of worship or talked with a visitor from a religious community.

How have they made their knowledge public?

Most children should have made a public display of their knowledge through talking and drawing. Some will have written short pieces. They should have listened attentively to visitors and behaved appropriately on visits.